*Wainwright's Favourite
Lakeland Mountains*

Also by A. Wainwright and Derry Brabbs
FELLWALKING WITH WAINWRIGHT

WAINWRIGHT ON THE PENNINE WAY

WAINWRIGHT'S COAST TO COAST WALK

WAINWRIGHT IN SCOTLAND

WAINWRIGHT ON THE LAKELAND MOUNTAIN PASSES

By A. Wainwright and Ed Geldard
WAINWRIGHT IN THE LIMESTONE DALES

Wainwright's Favourite Lakeland Mountains

A. WAINWRIGHT

with photographs by

DERRY BRABBS

Michael Joseph – London

MICHAEL JOSEPH LTD

Published by the Penguin Group
27 Wrights Lane, London W8 5TZ, England
Viking Penguin Inc., 375 Hudson Street, New York, New York 10014, USA
Penguin Books Australia Ltd, Ringwood, Victoria, Australia
Penguin Books Canada Ltd, 10 Alcorn Avenue, Toronto, Ontario, Canada M4V 3B2
Penguin Books (NZ) Ltd, 182-190 Wairau Road, Auckland 10, New Zealand

Penguin Books Ltd, Registered Offices, Harmondsworth, Middlesex, England

First published 1991

A CIP catalogue record for this book is available from the British Library

ISBN 0 7181 3370 6

Typeset in 10 on 12pt Linotron Galliard ITC
by Goodfellow & Egan Ltd, Cambridge
Colour reproduction by Anglia Graphics, Bedford
Printed and bound in Italy by L.E.G.O., Vicenza

The moral right of the author has been asserted

Contents

Introduction	vii	HAYSTACKS	103
BLENCATHRA	1	HELVELLYN	109
BOWFELL	21	HIGH STILE	123
CONISTON OLD MAN	31	HIGH STREET	131
CRINKLE CRAGS	41	HOPEGILL HEAD	143
DALE HEAD	51	LANGDALE PIKES	149
EEL CRAG	59	PILLAR	163
FAIRFIELD	65	SCAFELL	175
GLARAMARA	75	SCAFELL PIKE	187
GRASMOOR	81	SKIDDAW	203
GREAT GABLE	89	Index	213

Location maps by Chris Jesty
Illustration on half-title page: *The summit of Coniston Old Man*
Illustration on title page: *Great Gable and Sty Head from Scafell Pike*

Introduction

IN THE DAYS WHEN the early Victorians ventured upwards from the valleys, mountains were regarded with awe and considered dangerous, and it was the height of ambition to reach the summit of one of the better known, and then descend by the same route. The favoured practice was to ascend on ponyback in the company of a local man who served as guide and guarantor of success, and the popular objectives were those with prepared paths negotiable by ponies carrying human burdens, such as Helvellyn and Blencathra. But gradually over the years the fear and apprehension of the high places faded, ascents were made with the mutual support of companions, and then, a century ago, the first pioneers of rock-climbing came to Lakeland. Their adventures, documented by Owen Glynne Jones and photographed by the Abraham brothers, led others to the scenes of their exploits and opened the mountains for everyone.

The rock-climbers did not aim directly for the summits but wandered freely over the fells in search of crags worthy of their attention; they explored the lonely recesses and often travelled long distances on foot from their bases. They were the pioneers not only of rock-climbing but fellwalking too. Most visitors aspiring to reach a summit, however, still set their sights on a single mountain and, having achieved its top, retreated forthwith by the same route, proud to report their conquest to anyone who would listen.

Not until the last war, when the constraints of conflict were lifted and people could cast off their restricting chains and were able again to seek and enjoy the freedom of the hills and open spaces, did fellwalking as a pastime really spark the enthusiasm of the growing influx of visitors to Lakeland. On the fells there were no restrictions, no 'keep off' notices, and an eager new generation of walkers found exhilaration in wandering where they willed, no longer content merely to climb a mountain and come down again, no longer following only the trodden paths but prepared to make their own routes over rough ground. Strollers and ramblers in the valleys were converted and found greater pleasure in the high places.

After initial experience, most ardent fellwalkers discover their supreme enjoyment lies in traversing the high ridges that link the mountains together. The finest aspect of fellwalking is ridge walking; adrenalin runs high on the ridges.

Opposite *Grisedale Pike and Braithwaite*

Blencathra

2847 ft

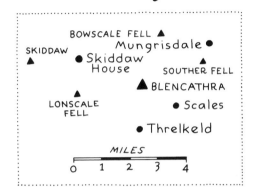

BLENCATHRA IS A PROUD name for a proud mountain and it is terrible to think that, some years ago, it seemed in danger of losing the lovely name that had been given to it by the early settlers. Although an inheritance from the distant past, the name had a mystical aura in harmony with the later popular conception, inspired by the Lake Poets, of the Lake District as a sanctuary of idyllic beauty and charm. Blencathra is an aloof but benevolent giant, a sheltering bulwark against northern storms, a provider of mineral wealth yet having an aspect so awesome and repelling that few men ventured into its wild fastnesses before the birth of fellwalking a century ago.

In Victorian times, however, the growing number of tourists attracted to the district by the eulogistical writings of the period, adopted and preferred an alternative name, one more prosaic, more descriptive of a feature of the mountain as seen prominently on the popular approach to Keswick from Penrith. From this easterly direction, the lofty skyline ridge appears as a curving depression between two summits, resembling a high saddle, and although not in view from other directions, the effect on imaginative minds was so pronounced that it earned for the mountain the alternative name of Saddleback – a good name had there not already been a better.

The new name became fashionable; some Victorian writers of guidebooks used it exclusively. Jenkinson's *Practical Guide to the English Lakes*, written 140 years ago (and which, incidentally, I consider to be the best guidebook to the district yet written) would have none of it: Saddleback was mentioned briefly but Blencathra was the author's clear preference. His was a lone voice. Towards the end of the last century and into the present, the name Blencathra was out of favour and often not even quoted as an option. The Ordnance Survey, however, compromised by naming it on their maps as 'Saddleback or Blencathra', obviously uneasy about abandoning the old name altogether but falling into line with the modern trend by adopting Saddleback as its first choice of name. Let us hope that one day soon, we shall see only the name Blencathra on the maps.

Opposite *Blencathra from Threlkeld Common*

So it happened that, with the post-war invasion of cars, coaches and caravans eroding the charm and tranquillity of Lakeland, in a world now more concerned with conflict and confrontation than with gentle living, the name of Blencathra became a casualty, falling from grace in favour of a name that reflected nothing of past glories and traditions. The couldn't-care-less brigade had arrived and old Blencathra must have writhed at their disrespect. The newcomers, however, did not influence locals who loved the mountain and preserved its name in the Blencathra Sanatorium and the Blencathra Foxhounds. John Peel would have been aghast at any attempt to change the name of his favourite pack to the Saddleback Foxhounds. Perish the thought!

Blencathra is a beautiful and inspiring name. Suburban householders all over the country have named their homes Blencathra. Nobody ever called his house Saddleback.

One effect of the growing pressure of traffic, the congestion of crowds and consequent commercialism in the valleys has been to induce discerning visitors who come as admirers of the natural beauty to take to the hills in search of peace and serenity, and there, in the high places, they find new perspectives and values in the silence of the summits. And Blencathra has become a firm favourite among the increasing army of fellwalkers and welcomes all who address him by his rightful name.

Blencathra from the Castlerigg Stone Circle

Blencathra from the east

Blencathra is a grand mountain standing aloof, independent, masculine, owing allegiance to no other, aware of its strategic importance as the cornerstone of Lakeland in the north-east, a sentinel charged with the duty of watching all who travel on the popular approach from Penrith.

For aeons nothing happened in the barren landscape Blencathra overlooked, then things slowly began to change. One day, thousands of years ago, he was surprised to see men constructing a stone circle on a low eminence two miles away, and then worshipping there; and subsequently greatly interested when another body of men built a number of stone huts and surrounding walls much nearer on a hillside directly opposite. Then, as the years went by, other men started the long process of clearing the swamps in the valley below and cultivating the land as pastures for their cattle. A narrow track formed along the base of the mountain and was travelled by packhorses and itinerant traders; cottages were built for miners who scraped the lower slopes for treasure. The biggest surprise of all happened in 1869 when men appeared in the fields below and laid a railway line, and surprise changed to amazement when, a century later, they came again and tore it up: they must be out of their minds, thought Blencathra; and Blencathra was right for today that railway would have made a fortune. In the meantime, the packhorses were replaced by machines that moved much faster and the track became a road which, in turn, as traffic rapidly increased, was abandoned in favour of a great new highway, the A66.

All these changes Blencathra has witnessed with a superior nonchalance. Things men do don't last. Blencathra is permanent, for ever.

The Southern Aspect

The A66 runs along the southern base of
Blencathra and travellers on this busy highway get
impressive and intimate sightings of the rising
buttresses and deep ravines of the lower slopes
but, due to foreshortening, only occasional glimpses
of the gaunt higher parts of the mountain. The most
popular viewpoint for photographers is Castlerigg
Stone Circle.

By far the best place for appraising the full extent
and unique characteristics of the mountain is
Threlkeld Common directly opposite. From here
there is a grandstand view of the whole southern
facade in detail, a scene of such massive proportions
that, even at this distance, a wide-angle lens will
be needed for the camera to encompass the full
picture, the tumbled walls of an Ancient British
village adding a foreground interest.

From the high ground of Threlkeld Common
the true stature of Blencathra is fully revealed, and
the masterly design of its natural architecture can
be appreciated. The lofty skyline of the summit
ridge is seen to be supported by five buttresses:
these are individually named as fells. The two
extremities, Blease Fell in the west and Scales Fell
in the east, have smooth, rounded slopes that
obviously offer easy routes of ascent. The three
intermediate buttresses are very different: each
rises from a broad base but becomes narrow and
emasculated in the higher reaches where they abut
the summit ridge. These middle buttresses offer
more direct ways to the top of the mountain but
fulfil their promise only after steep and arduous
climbing. The five buttresses are separated from
each other by deep watercourses in ravines choked
by stony debris: these are named, from the west,
as Blease Gill, Gate Gill, Doddick Gill and Scaley
Beck, all deceptively inviting. There are thus, on
the southern front alone, nine possible routes of
ascent, and no other mountain can offer such a
number and variety of ways to its top – which is a
good reason why this first chapter is longer than
any other in the book.

Blencathra's southern front from Threlkeld Common

BLEASE FELL

Blease Fell is the most westerly, bulkiest and least distinguished of the five buttresses supporting the summit ridge of Blencathra, having little of intrinsic interest and no feature of note apart from the cliffs of Knowe Crags that abruptly terminate the eastern edge of the fell. Seen from a distance, it is readily identified by the smooth surge of its skyline springing steeply from the depths of the valley of Glenderaterra Beck, the slope moderating gradually to the flat top of the fell. This is the longest unbroken slope in Lakeland.

Blease Fell is more often used as a way off the mountain than as a route of ascent, having the double merit of easy terrain and glorious prospect ahead with every step: the array of peaks around Borrowdale with Derwentwater a jewel in their midst makes a picture of supreme loveliness. But as an approach to the summit, Blease Fell has little to commend it. Starting from the road from Threlkeld to the former sanatorium without the advantage of a continuous path, the ascent is a tedious series of trials and errors to avoid low outcrops and marshy patches until the gradient eases and finally levels to reveal suddenly the slender summit ridge of the mountain directly ahead. Tedium is forgotten and replaced by excitement, the ridge is followed, skirting Knowe Crags and passing over Gategill Fell Top to the highest point of Blencathra with sensational views down on the right.

In a privileged location on the lower slopes of Blease Fell are the buildings of the former Blencathra Sanatorium, served by a tarred road. Time brings changes: the buildings are now occupied by the Lake District Planning Board and called Blencathra Centre. They are used for various holiday activities.

Blease Gill

BLEASE GILL

Blease Gill is a deep rift sharply dividing Blease Fell and Gategill Fell and, seen on a map, seems to offer a direct climb to the summit ridge. Initially it promises well; the route from Threlkeld is on a good track through a wooded dell with waterfalls, but beyond the trees the scene changes dramatically. The track ends at an abandoned lead mine, of which few traces remain, and ahead is a shattered wilderness of rocks and scree crowned high above by the cliffs of Knowe Crags, an arid desert, repelling and hostile. Gentle walkers will turn tail and flee the place, but hardy adventurers can proceed up the stony bed of the gill, following the main stream as it changes direction when the steep slope of Gategill Fell relents and, in an eerie silence, a canyon is entered that would make a fit setting for a wild west film before the walker scrambles up the narrow spine connecting Gategill Fell with the summit ridge. Here at last he may derive some pleasure from the climb. Blease Gill is a route to be recommended only with the strongest reservations: it is extremely rough underfoot, a struggle rather than a walk, and needs strong boots to combat stony terrain. It is a journey into a primitive wasteland where few venture.

Looking down on Gategill Fell from Gategill Fell Top

GATEGILL FELL

Rising directly above the fields of Threlkeld, Gategill Fell is the steepest of the five buttresses of Blencathra and the most arduous to ascend since there is no path and thick heather impedes upward progress. The climb starts from Blease Gill, rounds a corner of the intake wall that marks the limit of cultivation, and then, without the help of distinctive landmarks to provide direction, the steep slope above must be tackled. There follows a treadmill of unremitting steepness in a tangle of mature heather which, although pleasant to look upon, is a sore trial for most legs. Height is gained only slowly and ages seem to pass before the gradient eases at a knoll known as Knott Halloo, a fine vantage point probably so named by followers of the local foxhounds; it commands an aerial view of the wild recesses of Blease Gill far below. Now the toil of the ascent thus far is rewarded by less difficult conditions underfoot and exciting vistas all around. A relatively simple crossing, a stroll compared with what has gone before, leads to a prominent rock turret where the fellsides are seen to converge to form a narrow spine. This, after an initial descent, links unerringly with the summit ridge of the mountain, arriving there at Gategill Fell Top. The final stage of the ascent is rough but without hazards and, now assured of success, walkers will relish every step of the way. The highest point of Blencathra is within easy reach along the ridge.

Gategill Fell is no place for timid ramblers who prefer to travel on clear paths with signposts to point the way. The exhilaration of the upper reaches is won only after a desperate struggle up the uncompromising broad base of the fell with no semblance of pleasure, and the climb is best left to experienced fellwalkers. And Derry Brabbs.

Threlkeld Valley from Gate Gill

GATE GILL

Gate Gill is the best known of the deep channels that natural forces of weather, water and erosion have so savagely carved in the south face of Blencathra, best known not for tourist attractions, which are totally lacking, but because of its former reputation as a centre of mining activity. In the bed of the gill, encompassed by steep fellsides, was the old-established and productive Gate Gill Mine which for centuries employed the men of Threlkeld and contributed to the economic well-being of the village. The mineral mainly extracted was galena (lead sulphide) but the mine was abandoned long ago when it was unable to compete with cheaper foreign imports. Sad relics of the industry remain in a state of decay and neglect: crumbling earthworks and culverts are still to be seen and also the adits of the levels that were tunnelled deep into the heart of the mountain by pick and shovel in the early days before the use of gunpowder for blasting, a silent testimony to the hard labour of men who toiled for little reward.

Gate Gill is approached along a lane, constructed to serve the mine, turning off the old road through Threlkeld village and still in use as an access to the kennels of the Blencathra Foxhounds. It passes the site of the disused Woodend Mine, another casualty of economic circumstance. The lane ends at the narrow confines of the gill, a rough track continuing to the old workings. From this point, the summit of Blencathra is in view directly ahead, framed between the flanks of Gategill Fell and Hall's Fell and appearing to invite a direct ascent. But beyond the old workings, the way is pathless and rough and the wild downfall of rocks and scree from the summit too forbidding to contemplate. Escape from the gill can be made by ascending Middle Tongue, half left, on grass at first and emerging on the summit ridge near Gategill Fell Top after a steep scramble.

Gate Gill too is out of bounds for all but the very brave.

HALL'S FELL

Hall's Fell takes its name from Threlkeld Hall, which is set in fields on the other side of the A66. This is positively the best way up Blencathra; although it gets no mention in the pre-war guidebooks, it is a route of ascent which has gained in popularity in recent years. It is short in distance, direct, exciting, has glorious views in retrospect and striking scenes nearby. The greatest of its virtues is its unswerving course to the top of the mountain, scoring a bull's-eye by arriving precisely at the highest cairn. This is a route for connoisseurs to savour.

The climb starts from the end of the lane in Gate Gill, following a pretty path upwards through heather, a path that plays hide and seek, remaining hidden from below and revealing itself a few steps at a time, with charming zigzags to sustain interest during the ascent. Gradually the slope eases and the fell narrows to a ridge poised high between the depths of Gate Gill and Doddick Gill. The way forward is sheer delight, the path beckoning through and around outcrops, rocky turrets and natural gateways and steps. When I first came here I had to edge gingerly along a horizontal crack in a rock face at one point, but usage has bypassed the difficulty and there are now no impediments to hinder progress. This section is understandably named Narrow Edge; it is so exhilarating and enjoyable that there is a temptation to go back and do it again. At the end of this marvellous passage, the final stage of the climb is clearly seen ahead in the form of a slender ridge leading directly to the highest part of the mountain. It arrives unerringly at the cairn marking the summit of Blencathra, which the Ordnance Survey prefer to name Hall's Fell Top; in fact, modern maps now call the Summit Hallsfell Top.

Walkers who do this climb and keep diaries will record it as a red letter day. This is a route that lingers in the memory.

Gate Gill   *The final stage of Hall's Fell*

DODDICK GILL

I have made some harsh comments about some of the routes of ascent already described but their many difficulties are insignificant when compared with the terrors of Doddick Gill. This ravine carries a deep watercourse between the steep slopes of Hall's Fell and Doddick Fell and is so closely confined by impenetrable banks of dense heather that progress is only possible by a mad scramble up the bouldery bed of the descending stream. It is a desperate struggle where every step has to be planned and tested amongst the chaos of stones littering the cascading water, a way forward being gained only by involuntary slips and stumbles and wettings. All things come to an end, even Doddick Gill, and upon arriving at a confluence of streams at long last, bruised and dishevelled and questioning his sanity, the weary traveller has two chances of escape. Directly ahead and far above is the summit pyramid of Blencathra, quite obviously promising nothing but more discomfort and suffering, but by tackling the rough slope to the left, the ridge of Hall's Fell can be reached, giving a belated reward; alternatively, and much easier, a shorter climb to the right leads to the ridge of Doddick Fell, whence the summit of the mountain is quickly gained after negotiating the rocky crest of Doddick Fell Top.

Doddick Gill is for heroes only.

DODDICK FELL

I have never met or seen anyone on Doddick Fell, a circumstance of great appeal when the tourist route on nearby Scales Fell is awash with visitors. But apart from it qualities of quietness and seclusion, I rate Doddick Fell as second only to Hall's Fell as a route of ascent to Blencathra, the walking being comparatively easy and free from hazards: this is one of the few places on the south side of the mountain where striding out like a true fellwalker is possible.

A foothold on the fell is gained by following the intake wall from Scales after crossing Scaley Beck and then, by keeping to the height of land along a heathery ridge, the final rocks of Doddick Fell Top are negotiated and a simple walk leads to the summit.

Doddick Fell is a friend in an environment where so much of the terrain is hostile.

Doddick Gill

Looking west from Scales Fell

SCALES FELL

The time-honoured tourist route to the top of Blencathra is by way of Scales Fell, the most easterly of the southern buttresses of the mountain. In pioneering days, when ease of ascent was paramount, Scales Fell commended itself as a route free from difficulties; nowhere was excessively steep, and it provided the daring Victorian with a trouble-free route, especially for the ponies hired with guides to steady the nerves. Today there are no ponies and certainly no need for guides, generations of travellers on foot having smoothed a way upwards through thick grass following the line of the old pony route.

Scales is a hamlet, now bypassed by the new A66, two miles north-east of Threlkeld, and has access to the open fell. Initially the path made for the ponies goes to the right above the intake wall and then mounts the slope in a series of zigzags, above which, with the gradient easing, the engineered path ends. A beeline can then be made to the top of the fell in the imprints of countless walkers. This section is tedious, with nothing to see but thick grass all around, until one arrives at the head of a great hollow forming the gathering grounds of Scaley Beck, a watercourse dividing Doddick Fell and Scales Fell without pretensions as a route of ascent. The prospect forward is exciting: the turbulent landscape immediately west is revealed, the build-up of the mountain to its proud summit is seen as a grand design of ascending and narrowing ridges. At the top of Scales Fell, the summit ridge is joined for the final easy stage of the ascent, passing over Doddick Fell Top to the highest cairn. This section is of exceptional interest, disclosing the eastern side of the mountain as a large amphitheatre rimmed by the Saddle and Sharp Edge, their slopes falling steeply and roughly into a green hollow occupied by Scales Tarn.

Scales Fell offers the best route on a first visit to Blencathra, giving a good introduction to its unique topography. The more adventurous routes by way of Hall's Fell and Doddick Fell are strongly recommended for later occasions. Blease Fell is the best way down from the summit.

THE NORTHERN ASPECT

Blencathra is a Jekyll and Hyde mountain. Hyde is the savage southern front, a threatening monster difficult to placate and not inviting human companionship, a fearsome and repelling object without compassion for intruders. In complete contrast, Jekyll is the northern slope, of placid and urbane appearance, bland and expressionless, a friendly place but lacking in interest and excitement. Despite having a complete ground cover of grass, the northern slope has little to commend it as a route of ascent, being a dull trudge up a steady incline with no path to ease the passage through rough grass and nothing identifiable on the ridge ahead on which to focus the aim. There is a measure of relief in the retrospective view which expands as height is gained to include the vast expanse of the northern fells; John Peel loved to wander here, always on foot, with his pack of hounds and a company of dedicated followers in search of the elusive fox.

But the route is vindicated when the last few steps to the summit ridge suddenly, and with startling effect, bring into sight a breathtaking prospect of distant fells crowding around Borrowdale and Derwentwater: it is a vista of pure loveliness that comes as a blinding revelation after the tedious observance of underfoot greenery during the past hour. This is a wonderful moment, a fellwalking highlight.

Threlkeld is the best starting point for the northern slope, the road to the former sanatorium being continued beyond its terminus by a clear path rounding the eastern base of Blease Fell above the valley of Glenderaterra Beck which had relics of mining activity in and near the stream bed. After a mile of easy contouring, the path reaches a major tributary coming down on the right: this is Roughten Gill, the key to the ascent. The descending stream gives direction to the next stage but this is rough and pathless and, wherever seems convenient, its refreshing waters should be left and a beeline made for the ridge high on the right. It matters little where the ridge is reached, the highest point being an easy perambulation along it.

A feature of geological interest is to be found in the next watercourse after Roughten Gill, running parallel to it. This is Sinen Gill, one of the few places in the Skiddaw group of mountains, which are predominantly composed of slate, where an intrusion of granite occurs as a surface rock, forming huge boulders by a small waterfall.

THE EASTERN ASPECT

The architecture of the eastern flank of Blencathra has a distinctive character quite different from the other parts of the mountain. The summit is linked to a headland of steep rock, Foule Crag, by a slight depression known as the Saddle, this forming a gentle and graceful skyline-curve high above a vast hollow which in Wales would be called a cwm, in Scotland a corrie but in Lakeland usually has the name of combe or cove. This hollow is further encompassed by two arms of high ground springing from each end of the Saddle, Scales Fell and Sharp Edge, thus forming a lofty surround from which steep slopes fall into its grassy floor, the downfall of crags below the Saddle being particularly severe. Cradled in the depths of this great amphitheatre and sheltered by the encircling heights is the mountain's one sheet of water, Scales Tarn, its issuing stream giving direction to the only easy line of escape from the combe as it rushes down a rough channel to join the Glenderamackin; this is the river that defines effectively but erratically the eastern boundary of the mountain.

Above *View north from Sinen Gill to Caldbeck Fells*   Below *The valley of Glenderaterra Beck*

The white cross   Opposite *Sharp Edge, looking east*

THE SADDLE

Although poised high above a shattered landscape and reached only by arduous effort, the Saddle provides the easiest walking surface on the mountain, a simple stroll on excellent turf.

Walkers who reach the depression of the Saddle will be curious to learn about a man-made and unique landmark they will see there. A cross has been laid out on the ground, composed of white crystallised stones of high quartz content. Locals believe it was originally intended to be a memorial to a walker who died when walking on the mountain, but its initial small size has been extended to its present proportions of 16ft x 10ft. A Threlkeld man, Harold Robinson, climbed Blencathra, his favourite mountain, hundreds of times and, on each visit, he added a few more stones from the nearby veins of quartzite. The cross may now be regarded as a memorial to Mr Robinson too.

SHARP EDGE

Sharp Edge is well named: it juts from the main mass of the mountain below the Saddle as a narrow spine of rock bristling with vertebrae in the form of pinnacles and towers of intimidating aspect. In some ways it resembles the better-known Striding Edge on Helvellyn but it is shorter and, if the crest is traversed from end to end without deviation, is much more difficult and dangerous. To the early Victorian pioneers, Sharp Edge was a terrifying place and its crossing perilous; this is not so today if advantage is taken of a pedestrian path formed by the passage of many boots on the northern side of the crest and a few feet below it. The sides of Sharp Edge are steep and in places precipitous so that it is advisable to walk circumspectly and keep strictly to the trodden path. There is one minor difficulty at the point where the Edge abuts the fellside, where a small tilted slab has to be negotiated: here the ultra-cautious walker, decorum abandoned, will prefer to shuffle across the impasse in a sitting position. Otherwise there is nowadays nothing to fear when traversing the Edge in fair conditions; if sheathed in ice, it is far better avoided.

Sharp Edge is exciting, exhilarating and a memorable adventure. Of Blencathra's many delights for the fellwalker it is supreme.

Scales Tarn

SCALES TARN

The immense hollow on the eastern flank, scooped out of the fellside as though by a giant bulldozer, was shaped by a retreating glacier in millenia long past, leaving a debris of crags and scree, a petrified desert without life or movement, pervaded by an awesome stillness. This dead landscape is relieved of its solemnity by a sheet of water, Scales Tarn, deeply inurned below a crescent of impending crags and steep declivities and serving as a natural reservoir for the drainage from the slopes of the recess. The tarn occupies a pleasant grassy basin but under a grey sky appears sullen and gloomy and rather sinister; only the lapping of water on the shores and the gurgle of the outflow into Scales Beck disturb the profound silence.

Sir Walter Scott in his *Bridal of Triermain* described the surface of the tarn as a 'black mirror' in which 'you may spy the stars while noontide lights the sky', words well larded with poetic licence and having no substance in fact. I was reminded of his flight of fancy one sunny day in high summer when, looking down on the tarn from the heights above, I saw the surface rippled by a light breeze with every little wavelet carrying a sparkle of sunlight: it needed little imagination to interpret the sight as the reflection of a galaxy of stars. Sir Walter was vindicated.

The eastern features may be linked in a circuitous route of ascent of Blencathra. A good path leaves Scales above the intake wall and continues into the valley of the River Glenderamackin until reaching Scales Beck, which is then followed upstream to Scales Tarn. From here the slope to the right leads up to Sharp Edge; this is traversed to reach the Saddle on a much-eroded path, finally passing the white cross to the summit.

Sharp Edge is the magnet that attracts many walkers to this interesting route.

THE RIVER GLENDERAMACKIN

Of all the watercourses draining the fells of Lakeland, the most wayward and erratic in its direction of flow is the River Glenderamackin which, by an unusual lie of the land, is forced into a tortuous channel of twists and U-turns to all points of the compass before being allowed to travel sedately.

The valley of the River Glenderamackin

The river takes shape below the watershed between Blencathra and Bannerdale Crags and at first aims resolutely south-east until deflected east by a low barrier of land to the greater obstacle of Souther Fell, an impasse with only one line of escape: due north along the valley of Bannerdale. Only when the slopes of Souther Fell decline to valley level is the river permitted to turn east again, reaching Mungrisdale in a pretty glen. From there, no longer constrained by steep contours, it follows a course of its own choice, gently meandering along the eastern base of Souther Fell and enters the lovely valley of the River Greta, just south-west of Threlkeld; here it joins the company of other streams and finally augments the waters of the River Derwent.

SOUTHER FELL

Souther Fell is almost wholly encircled by the River Glenderamackin which defines the eastern boundary of Blencathra, and although having the appearance of a separate fell and being of considerable altitude, must be regarded as an offshoot of the parent mountain. Souther Fell, earlier known as Souter or Soutra Fell, is the last bastion of high ground in north-east Lakeland and has a wide outlook over the Eden Valley to the distant Pennines. Otherwise it merits little mention except for the remarkable legend associated with it.

On a summer evening in the mid-eighteenth century, a farm labourer living nearby was amazed and startled to see a continuous line of soldiers, some on horseback, marching along the top of the fell in an unending procession until darkness hid their movements. His story was not believed but when, on a later occasion, the phenomenon reappeared he called out his neighbours to witness it. Twenty-six local inhabitants of sober repute whose veracity was not in doubt attested to the indisputable fact that they too had seen troops of marching soldiers silhouetted against the sky on the top of the fell. What they saw must have been a mirage, an apparition, and the only explanation advanced by learned men who investigated the circumstances was that a curious refraction of light had caused a vaporous reflection of Prince Charlie's Highland rebels who, it was discovered later, had been exercising on the west coast of Scotland the same evening. The year was 1745.

Opposite *Blencathra from Souther Fell*   Above *Skiddaw from the summit of Blencathra*

The Summit: 2847 FT

The Ordnance Survey prefer to give the name of Hall's Fell Top to the highest point of Blencathra and, indeed, it is situated precisely where Hall's Fell abuts on the summit ridge. But those who reach this exalted peak do not record in their diaries 'Climbed Hall's Fell Top today': they say 'Climbed Blencathra today'.

An untidy pile of stones marks the summit and is surrounded by a greensward that invites rest and a contemplation of the magnificent panorama revealed on all sides.

The views are far reaching, extending to distant horizons except where interrupted by the greater bulk of nearby Skiddaw. Over the lesser northern fells is seen the Solway plain and eastwards, in a wealth of detail, is the Penrith countryside and the fertile Eden Valley backed by the highest of the Pennines with Cross Fell overtopping the range. Towards the south, the fells of Lakeland start to erupt from their lovely valleys, culminating in the massive upthrust of Helvellyn and its supporting satellites. But it is in the arc between south and south-west that attention will be mostly rivetted: here is a tumult of peaks so crowded together that the identification of each can only be made by fellwalkers with a long and intimate knowledge of the district. This is a compelling vista, a picture of infinite beauty, and in its midst like a jewel in a prickly crown, is Derwentwater.

Samuel Taylor Coleridge expressed the feelings of his contemporaries when he wrote of Blencathra's perilous height and tyrannous winds. Attitudes change with the times. The mountain is no longer a fearful place where only the brave venture accompanied by guides. It has become a popular objective for active walkers of all ages.

I climbed Blencathra every Sunday in the winter of 1960/61 and never once saw another human being. I had the mountain to myself, discovering its secrets and hidden recesses, and on the summit was a king on his throne. Treated with respect, Blencathra was a rough but genial giant who seemed to welcome my weekly visits. We forged a bond of friendship that has remained strong ever since.

Bowfell

2960 ft

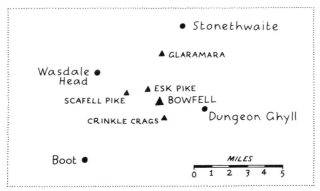

THE ORDNANCE SURVEY HAVE always preferred on their maps to express the name of this noble mountain as two words, Bow Fell, and are correct in doing so if only in the interests of consistency since all other heights in the Lake District which have Fell as part of their names, such as Place Fell, Harter Fell, Lingmoor Fell, are invariably written and spoken as two separate words and never telescoped into one. Bowfell is the exception, possibly because the two words flow easily together in speech; the dalesfolk's local pronunciation being Bowfle. Since the turn of the century all writers have adopted the spelling of Bowfell.

The most arresting and spectacular feature of the valley of Great Langdale is the stark profile of the Langdale Pikes, an awesome scene forever remembered by visitors. Less obtrusive is the majestic peak at the head of the valley, the dominant height on a lofty, encircling skyline, its rocky summit pyramid set on a plinth of grassy slopes. This is Bowfell, unassuming and rather withdrawn from public attention yet a commanding presence. It oversees a wild domain, a tangled landscape of abrupt rises and falls with a distant horizon largely formed by the turbulent skyline of a wide-ranging array of high fells – it is a primeval scene of desolation crudely fashioned by natural forces, littered with the debris of creation, and relieved only by an expanse of sea and the green straths of radiating valleys.

The easy approach gives no hint of the ruggedness of the summit nor the spectacular features hidden from sight amongst the uppermost rocks. Walkers who adhere to the well-trodden tourist path do not see the true glory of the mountain and only those who deviate and explore earn the best rewards from the ascent. Bowfell's unique secrets are locked away amongst its cliffs and crags but the key is available to those who are prepared to venture forth and make intimate acquaintance with the unique features waiting to be discovered.

For all who reach the top cairn on Bowfell in clear weather, there is ample recompense for their efforts in the magnificent panorama that is suddenly revealed. In that supreme moment, one can fully appreciate the grandeur of Bowfell.

Opposite *Bowfell*

Mickleden and The Band

THE BAND

The royal road to the top of Bowfell, the route invariably followed for the ascent, is provided by one long shoulder of the mountain furnished with a green carpet that springs suddenly from the level pastures of Stool End and rises gradually to the summit pryamid between the side valleys of Oxendale and Mickleden.

This grassy incline has an open invitation for visitors to Great Langdale amounting almost to a welcome. It is, moreover, the only obvious way to the top, no others seeming practicable, and consequently suffers much foot-traffic. The grassy carpet becomes frayed and worn by the passage of many boots. The walking, however, is easy although unexciting, interest being sustained by the impressive views of Pike o'Stickle and Pike o'Blisco across the enclosing valleys. The Mickleden flank has a fringe of crags, avoided by the rising path, but otherwise The Band is innocuous, posing no more danger than a children's playground and, being equally safe in descent, is also commonly used as a way down. In fact, The Band is the easiest mile of fell in the whole surround of Great Langdale.

At the top of The Band, however, the terrain becomes rougher and steeper and the usual tourist path veers to the left into the depression of the Three Tarns before turning sharply upwards and becoming badly eroded on the final stage to the summit cairn.

There is an interesting alternative approach to The Band, reaching its crest at mid-height. This route relieves the tedium of the ascent, offers mild excitement and, because of its distractions, adds an hour to the climb. By walking along Oxendale from Stool End and passing through the rocky jaws of this valley, a great gash in the fellside on the right is revealed. This is Hell Gill and in the lower part of its gloomy depths is the splendid waterfall of Whorneyside Force, not easy to reach but worth a close visit. Then a steep scramble up the side of the gill leads to kinder slopes and a meeting with the path along the top of The Band. This is not a route for genteel walkers but adventurous spirits will enjoy it.

THE LINKS

Walkers on the steep section of the path rising from the depression of Three Tarns will need to concentrate their attention on negotiating the sliding scree underfoot but, pausing, may notice a long line of cliffs alongside. These cliffs, imperfectly seen from the path and better viewed from Shelter Crags beyond the tarns, are unique in Lakeland: they are split by a dozen parallel gullies, alike in pattern as though scraped out by a gigantic comb with the power of a bulldozer. The gullies, known as the Links of Bowfell, are choked by boulders and spew out fans of scree.

The Links drop sharply from the summit plateau and, before the path to the cairn became well trodden, constituted a dangerous trap for walkers descending from the top, their gaping openings seeming to offer quick ways down, a menace that gradually disappeared as the path became more distinct. I once spent an unhappy hour getting down one of these gullies, a frightening experience amongst shifting boulders. Venturesome walkers should not regard the Links as a challenge: they are a potential source of accident and should be avoided.

The Links of Bowfell

The Climbers' Traverse

THE CLIMBERS' TRAVERSE

The usual tourist path to the top of Bowfell is the best to follow, without deviation, for walkers of a timid disposition, but there is another way through the labyrinth of rock formations below the summit for active walkers who suffer bruises lightly. Where the path veers left at the top of The Band, a scramble up the rough ridge directly ahead leads to a track turning off to the right along a horizontal shelf flanked by a line of cliffs. This is the Climbers' Traverse, devised as a time-saving short cut by rock-climbers bound for Bowfell Buttress and for a long time kept a secret from ordinary

mortals. Walking on this track is easy but pulses quicken at the sight of the imposing rock architecture immediately ahead. Down on the right and far below is seen the head of Mickleden and Rossett Gill, but attention is rivetted on the surrounding intimate scene, an awe-inspiring succession of naked crags, lofty towers and pinnacles, forming an insurmountable barrier with no apparent breach in its defences. After the friendliness of The Band, the surroundings are decidedly hostile but pose no danger to walkers endowed with common sense.

The waterspout on Cambridge Crag

The first vertical cliffs are those of Flat Crags, the reasons for this contradictory name being apparent later. Then, beyond a tumble of boulders, rises the impressive bastion of Cambridge Crag, identified by a waterspout gushing from its lower rocks alongside the path, a fountain of liquid refreshment, a bonus all the more welcome for being unexpected. The track then descends into a wide scree gully bounded by the great tower of Bowfell Buttress, a huge pinnacle of rock soaring into the sky and a favourite haunt of cragsmen.

To reach the summit of the mountain from the Traverse is a problem that can be solved by either of two routes: by struggling up the wide scree slope to easy ground above, but without deriving any pleasure from doing so; or, preferably, by negotiating the tumble of boulders to a shallow crack dividing Flat Crags and Cambridge Crag and following this upwards. On this ascent the top of Flat Crags is seen to be formed of a great slab of rock lightly crevassed and tilted at an easy angle, hence the name. At the top a field of boulders, some unstable and needing care, is crossed to the summit cairn. Both routes involve rough scrambling and any pretensions to elegance of movement must be discarded.

The Climbers' Traverse introduces spectacular rock formations denied to pedestrians on the tourist path. It is an excursion into a secret hidden realm of natural wonders.

The Great Slab, Flat Crags

ROSSETT GILL

Sooner or later, and usually sooner than later, every fellwalker in Lakeland is confronted by Rossett Gill, the greatest obstacle on the popular high-level crossing between Great Langdale and Wasdale. The gill forms a distinctive part of the northern boundary of Bowfell, being clearly defined by the channel of stones issuing from its narrow upper confines and sprawling over the fellside below, a ladder of rocky debris 1200 feet in height that sorely tries the patience and taxes the energy of everyone climbing up or down it. Its ascent is arduous, its descent a despairing search for firm footing. I do not think I have ever heard anyone speak but ill of Rossett Gill; it is a place without charm, made noisy by clattering stones and guttural oaths. To make matters worse, thousands of boots have destroyed the ground so much that, to persuade walkers to keep out of the dangerous upper section, the Lake District wardens have made a bypass half-way by improving a thin track linking with the old pony route.

Rossett Gill is not a source of sentimental memories, but I am always touched by the sad reminder of an event that happened two hundred years ago. A packwoman carrying supplies to the Langdale farms perished here, and near a grassy knoll is a simple cross of stones laid on the ground to mark her grave. I have never disclosed the exact site of this plot of hallowed ground to avoid disturbance – and I hope this will always be respected.

I had toiled up and down Rossett Gill dozens of times before noticing on an old map that formerly there had been a pony route which avoided Rossett Gill entirely by means of a circuitous track along the lower slopes of Bowfell. I found it, neglected and forgotten but still distinct for most of the way and still indicated by a few hoary and ancient cairns. Interesting features remained: from near the top of Rossett Gill a grooved path, obviously engineered, led down the open fellside, straight as a die, to a pretty waterslide coming off Bowfell with a causeway provided to ease the crossing.

The hidden sheepfold on the old pony route

Looking north-east to Blencathra

The path then continued, marked by cairns, and descended grassy slopes into Mickleden, crossing the beck to join the valley path to Great Langdale, the later stages of the pony route having gone to seed and become untraceable. Near the waterslide and unseen from the valley is a sheepfold reputedly built to hide the cattle and sheep during the days of the border raids.

The old pony route was a valuable discovery. Never again did I struggle up or down Rossett Gill.

ORE GAP

The only feasible alternative to The Band as a route of ascent to Bowfell from Great Langdale is more circuitous, twice the distance and involves a confrontation with the unfriendly Rossett Gill before some good scenery makes compensations in its later stages.

The route goes along Mickleden and climbs or circumvents Rossett Gill to its grassy top which is then revealed as a pass, the ground beyond descending to the outlet of an impressive mountain tarn, the issuing stream falling away into Langstrath. This is Angle Tarn which occupies a hollow backed by the craggy heights of Hanging Knotts, a spur of Bowfell. It appears gloomy and sinister when under a ceiling of cloud and offers a sparkling invitation only in warm sunlight. The route skirts its far side, heading for an obvious break in the skyline directly ahead between Bowfell and Esk Pike. This is Ore Gap, crossed by a path flanking the two mountains and notable for the red subsoil which the well-trodden path exposes, indicating the presence of a vein of hematite, hence the name. The path leftwards leads easily to the summit of Bowfell above the declivities of Hanging Knotts and Bowfell Buttress, an interesting and visually exciting line of approach to the ultimate cairn.

Bowfell from Eskdale

THE SUMMIT: 2960 FT

The highest point of Bowfell is indicated by a large cairn set on a plinth of angular rocks offering little comfort to visitors who wish to rest in leisurely contemplation of the scene around, yet few who arrive on a day of clear visibility will regret the effort of getting there. The view is magnificent, a far-reaching and comprehensive panorama of mountains and fells in silent assembly, range succeeding range like waves of a tempestuous sea and extending into the far distance. A sombre plateau, a choke of boulders and outcrops abruptly ended by plunging crags. Most impressive is the massive uplift of the Scafells nearby, seen end to end across the deep gulf of Upper Eskdale, Crinkle Crags displays its ruggedness a short mile away, and the Langdale Pikes, although dwarfed by Bowfell's superior height, still contrive to appear pugnacious. But not everything in sight is harsh mountainous terrain. There are fair valleys to look upon: eastwards, Great Langdale is seen as from an aeroplane, its lovely curves leading the eye to the silver waters of Windermere and the Pennines far beyond; northwards the green ribbon of Langstrath breaches the tawny fells on its way to Borrowdale, and to the south-west Eskdale presents a glorious picture on its winding course to the sea, the estuary of the River Esk adding a bright halo to a pageant of colour.

Many people regard Bowfell's summit as the finest viewpoint in Lakeland. In my opinion, it does not quite qualify for that honour, the Scafell range hiding from view the exciting western fells beyond with only the tips of Great Gable and Pillar peeping over the skyline rather reproachfully. Not in dispute, however, is the claim that the summit of Bowfell is one of the most rewarding mountain tops in the district.

THE ESKDALE FLANK

Seen from Eskdale in the south, Bowfell assumes the shape of a symmetrical pyramid, its graceful outline contrasting sharply with the ruggedness of the other peaks around the head of the valley. The open aspect of the mountain as viewed from Great Langdale is not repeated here, its full stature being concealed by intervening foothills. Nevertheless, on this side Bowfell has distinction and dominance, presiding over a tangled landscape rich in variety and colour, a vista of beauty enhanced by a lovely river and waterfalls; indeed, the approach from Eskdale, a delightful valley, is amongst the grandest walks in Lakeland.

At close quarters, however, the Eskdale flank directly below the summit presents a sight to repel even the toughest of walkers, a wilderness of boulders poised at a steep angle, a haven for foxes maybe, but offering no comfort at all for visitors on two legs. A direct climb to the apex of the pyramid is out of the question. This is Bowfell's no-man's-land. A less hazardous way to the top must be found.

Every step of the way from Brotherilkeld, with the River Esk a charming companion, is a joy to tread and beyond the quaint Lingcove Bridge the beauty of the journey is sustained as the path rises alongside the leaping waterfalls of Lingcove Beck to the vast natural amphitheatre of Green Hole, from which the slopes of Bowfell rise in increasing steepness to a petrified cataract of boulders below the summit. Avoiding the obvious difficulties of a direct ascent, the path climbs steadily along the stony lower flanks of Crinkle Crags to reach easier ground, passing below the Links to arrive at the Three Tarns where here the much-trodden route by way of The Band can be joined.

The Scafell range from Bowfell

Coniston Old Man

2633 ft

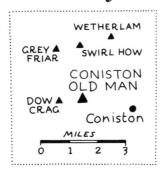

I ONCE WROTE, in a spasm of exuberance, that the Old Man is to Coniston as the Matterhorn is to Zermatt, a gross exaggeration, of course. Yet there is the same affinity between mountain and village: one without the other is unthinkable, and both are integral in the public's image. People go to Zermatt to see the Matterhorn, and a few to climb it. People go to Coniston not to feast their eyes on the Old Man but when he comes into sight, some strange magnetism impels many to make the ascent. Indeed, climbing the Old Man is almost a ritual for those staying in Coniston. The mountain is within sight every day, dominating the scene, offering a mute invitation to all. Many accept: there are few days in the year when the Old Man does not play host to visitors, and in summer the blazed path to the top carries processions of pedestrians young and old, and there is often a noisy congregation on the summit. The Old Man doesn't mind – although he would really prefer to be left in peace to lick his wounds.

And his wounds, all inflicted by man, are much in evidence. Coniston Old Man has been more cruelly exploited than any other mountain in Lakeland. For centuries, he has been the centre of industrial activity and the resulting scars are still vividly obvious. His flanks have been disfigured by tunnels and shafts which were sunk in a search for mineral wealth, and mutilated by quarries searching for the slate whose colour and quality have made it justly famous. Although all this industry has obviously contributed to the economy of the village, it has been at the expense of much devastation. It is only because the Old Man is such a proud mountain that he has not succumbed to man's exploitations.

The mountain forms an immense natural barrier sheltering the village from western storms, another of his benefactions, and ends the high ground of Lakeland in the south, having a far-reaching view of the sea and a lengthy stretch of coastline. To the north are the grand fells, range succeeding range into the haze of distance. The Old Man stands aloof, forming with his satellite neighbours a compact mass to which, as befits his status as the undisputed overlord of the Coniston domain, he holds the key.

Opposite *Coniston Old Man from Red Dell Head*

Coppermines Valley

Until 1974 the Coniston Fells occupied the north-western extremity of Lancashire but in that year, as part of a local government reorganisation, the bureaucrats of Whitehall decreed by a stroke of the pen that they should be included in the new county of Cumbria. Many of the changes then made were resented because they had little regard to historical associations and local traditions, but this one did make sense, bringing the whole of the Lake District within a single boundary.

ASCENTS FROM CONISTON

Ascents of the Old Man are not inspired by scenes of natural beauty which are sadly lacking: all routes from Coniston lead upwards through areas of industrial devastation. As Mallory said of Everest, you climb it because it is there.

On busy days the only instruction needed is to follow the crowds but even then there is a choice of routes. The pleasantest way leaves the Sun Hotel and passes through fields and trees alongside Church Beck before turning away to join the quarry road for a dusty climb to the workings, which one passes round for the final steep pull to the top. Another route follows the tarmac road uphill past the site of the defunct railway station to the open moorland where the quarry road going off to the right is followed; this is joined by the footpath route for the final stage to the summit.

Another route, unfrequented and with a cast-iron guarantee that no other walkers will be seen until the summit is reached and therefore particularly suitable for those of an anti-social disposition, goes ahead from the open moorland on the Walna Scar Road, turning off at Boo Tarn in favour of a quarry road coming down from the re-vitalised Bursting Stone Quarry; above this an enchanting track zigzags up the open fellside to join the south ridge to the summit.

COPPERMINES VALLEY

On a flat shelf of the mountain above the village, reached by a road alongside Church Beck (which has a splendid waterfall), is the so-called Coppermines Valley. Here, enclosed by the descending streams of Levers Water Beck and Red Dell Beck, is the accumulated debris of a centuries-old copper mining activity, long abandoned. On the fellside around are the old levels and shafts and ancillary works, left to decay when the miners downed their tools for the last time. Since then, the years have taken their toll and the levels are now ruinous, unsafe and extremely dangerous, many of the gaping holes in the ground being unprotected: children and dogs must be kept on a tight leash here.

This is an area I found totally fascinating to explore, tracing all the sources of activity on old maps. There is the silence of death in these old workings, and sadness: it is a test of the imagination to visualise the conditions in which forgotten men scraped a living from the ground. A recent proposal to establish a leisure centre on the site with all the fun of the fair was rejected by the planning authority. Quite right: you don't build on a graveyard.

One of the mine buildings is now a Youth Hostel, and a terrace of miners' cottages, once ruinous, has been restored as holiday homes. Let the rest remain as an industrial museum.

LEVERS WATER

Levers Water is a large expanse occupying a wild hollow in the hills above Coppermines Valley, a natural tarn brought into service as a reservoir by the erection of a massive dam to contain and control supplies to the mines. Although the need ceased with the closing of the mines, the dam remains serviceable, the outflow passing through a tunnel to emerge as Levers Water Beck. The issuing stream descends steeply in cascades and cataracts, and from it water cuts have been skilfully engineered to contour the fellsides and serve outlying mines.

Near the dam is Simon's Nick: this is an amazing sight where a huge vertical slice of rock has been carved out of a crag, one of the many wonders in this interesting industrial complex.

Levers Water

Boo Tarn

BOULDER VALLEY

Low Water Beck joins Levers Water Beck beyond the Youth Hostel and if followed upstream brings into view a green hollow littered by large boulders fallen from the heights above. One of immense girth with vertical walls that defy access to its top to all but rock-climbers is called the Pudding Stone.

The beck issues from Low Water, a tarn higher up the fellside and this may be reached by a steep and pathless scramble alongside. Low Water, in shy seclusion and not often visited, nestles in the lap of the Old Man who personally overlooks this last gem in his tortured crown and is as yet undisturbed by commercial interests. A shattered tumble of scree and crags falls steeply from the summit into the waters of the tarn, barring a direct ascent, but nearby is the tourist path and this should be used for the final stage of the climb to the top.

WALNA SCAR ROAD

An ancient highway skirts the southern slopes of the Old Man to link Coniston with the Duddon Valley, taking advantage of the only relatively easy crossing between them but even so it climbs to a height of almost 2000 feet. Although classed as a road and once in common use as a passage for horses and carts, it fell into disuse as a route for communications and commerce last century, a casualty of improved transport facilities. Its rough unmetalled surface has degenerated through neglect into a narrow path, still well defined but of use to travellers on foot only. The approaches have been given a tarmac surface at both ends but the miles between have gone to seed.

History has been made here. On the open moor near Boo Tarn, a reedy pool beside the road, the antiquities and artifacts of a Bronze Age settlement have been discovered and, spanning the centuries, in 1954 a schoolboy photographed a flying saucer passing overhead and produced a picture to prove it.

The summit of Coniston Old Man

THE SUMMIT: 2633 FT

I suppose it is true to say that the summit of the Old Man, more so than of any other mountain top in Lakeland, attracts a majority of visitors who do not profess to be regular fellwalkers and are not even lovers of the hills. They struggle to the top, often ill-shod and ill-equipped because the climb is the recognised thing to do when based in Coniston. Infants and old age pensioners, and all ages between, are commonly represented in the triumphant congregation on the top and it is a popular venue for school parties.

The blazed path from the village ends after a steep and stony final section on a mound bearing the imprint of many boots in the trampled grass amongst embedded and outcropping flakes of slate. Surmounting all is a large stone platform used as a viewing station and bearing a well-built cairn. On the ground nearby an Ordnance Survey column completes the summit furniture.

As befits the Old Man's terminal position in the south of the district, there is a glorious seascape in view, ranging over the estuaries of the rivers Kent, Leven and Duddon and a wide expanse of Morecambe Bay beyond. It is in this direction that most eyes turn, the viewing platform significantly providing an uninterrupted panorama seaward, and shouts of glee proclaim the sighting of Blackpool Tower and the Isle of Man. To east and west also there are far-reaching prospects of colourful foothills declining to the coast in a pageant of sylvan loveliness enhanced by lakes and tarns, ten in all, of which Coniston Water is most prominent. It is seen full length in an exquisite setting. The view in the northern arc, obstructed by the cairn and therefore less appealing to many who reach the summit, is of great appeal to the fellwalker since it includes all the major heights of Lakeland in a thrilling array, an inspiring vision, a challenge.

The Old Man commands an unsurpassed panorama.

Dow Crag with Goats Water

DOW CRAG

The most spectacular feature of the Coniston Fells, within sight from the Old Man and less than a mile away, is Dow Crag, a fearful precipice falling from a small peaked summit to a steep slope littered by boulders and scree above the dark depths of Goat's Water in a wild hollow at its base, the whole a tremendous downfall of rock and debris a thousand feet in height. The precipice is formed by five buttresses divided by cavernous gullies, all near vertical and manifestly unassailable by ordinary mortals.

Second only to Scafell Crag as the most formidable cliff in the district, Dow Crag saw the birth of Lakeland rock-climbing when a group of enthusiastic adventurers from Barrow and the Furness area made regular assaults on the crag in the closing years of the last century; at that time, they were assisted in their approach by the train service to Coniston. They established a network of routes that have remained firm favourites with the climbing fraternity ever since.

The summit is an airy perch on a pile of rocks immediately above the abyss and is easily reached along the ridge from Walna Scar or from the Old Man by way of Goat's Hause. The western slopes, in complete contrast, descend easily and without incident to the farmsteads of the Duddon Valley.

THE CONISTON HORSESHOE

From the summit of the Old Man the main ridge of the Coniston Fells is seen extending northwards at a high level, offering an invitation to walkers with time to spare to pursue it to its abrupt termination on Swirl How. Here a link can be made with a parallel ridge descending to Coniston, making possible a horseshoe expedition with few difficulties and many rewards. It can be recommended in any conditions except darkness.

A shallow depression is crossed from the top of the Old Man to the next summit, Brim Fell, which has a larger cairn than it deserves, there being nothing here of immediate interest. The ridge then descends gradually to a pronounced gap, Levers Hause, and climbs the facing slope, skirting the edge of Little How Crags. Looking back here it will be seen that the ridge thus far is scarped on the Coniston side throughout its length, the only feasible access to it being the tourist path to the Old Man; the western slopes, however, are grassy sheep pastures going down to a green hollow containing Seathwaite Tarn, a reservoir with relics of former mining activity at its head.

Little How Crags are succeeded by Great How Crags, both falling in steep cliffs to a desolate recess known as the Prison, but they are passed almost unnoticed by walkers on the ridge which ends in an easy promenade to a cairn on Swirl How. Here further progress forward is brought to an abrupt halt by a sudden collapse of the ground ahead into the Greenburn Valley far below, rivers of scree falling from a fringe of cliffs in a chaotic tumble.

The summit of Swirl How

Above *Wetherlam from Swirl How*   Below *View from Wetherlam*

Swirl How is a counterpart of the Old Man, both having the same function of buttressing the ridge between them and they are similar in altitude, Swirl How having the advantage by a few inches only. In other respects they are very different; the Old Man is the object of public patronage but Swirl How has few visitors and remains quiet and undisturbed; for this very reason it appeals more to those who prefer to enjoy their mountain experiences in solitude. The view from Swirl How is as good as that from the Old Man, although the coastal view is sacrificed for the greater detail of the surrounding fells. The nearest, Great Carrs, still carries the wreckage of a wartime aeroplane disaster.

From the summit of Swirl How the next objective of the horseshoe walk, Wetherlam, is seen a mile away to the east.

From the top of Swirl How, a path goes off sharp right and leads down the rough ridge of Prison Band to the depression of Swirl Hawse, where tired legs can avoid further climbing by descending an easy slope to Levers Water and then more steeply to the Coppermines Valley and Coniston. But this is cheating. To continue the horseshoe walk, the facing slope must be climbed to the subsidiary summit of Black Sails, continuing thence to the top of Wetherlam, which now lies directly ahead.

Wetherlam is a bulky fell; it commands a lovely view over Little Langdale and is especially rich in lakes and tarns, no fewer than fifteen sheets of water being visible. Northwards, there is a crowd of peaks ranging to far horizons. The extensive view is the glory of Wetherlam; its shame is its pockmarked lower slopes, ruthlessly exploited in a search for mineral wealth and left abandoned for nature to heal. But nature cannot refurbish man-made tunnels driven into cliffs or open shafts in the ground, and these decaying evidences of former mining activity are still plain to see. There appear to be almost a hundred gaping holes in the sides of Wetherlam, traps for the unwary walker.

These hazards do not present themselves on the horseshoe walk, however, which from the summit turns south along the declining ridge of Lad Stones to reach the Coppermines Valley and Coniston, bringing to an end a splendid expedition.

TILBERTHWAITE GILL

Before the cars and the crowds came to the Lake District, Tilberthwaite Gill was the special preserve of discerning admirers of natural beauty who jealously guarded its treasures and respected and appreciated efforts made to maintain its wonderful appeal for the enjoyment of visitors.

This gill, on the lower eastern slopes of Wetherlam, was once a showplace of unique charm that has since fallen from grace. It is a delightful oasis in an arid waste of spoil-heaps from an adjoining disused quarry where a cascading stream rushes through a ravine between confining rock walls. There is no room for a path, but formerly help was provided for an exciting passage upstream by ladders and steps, balconies and plank bridges to where it emerged from a hole tunnelled in a cliff, a short journey in an exquisite setting of rare loveliness overhung by trees.

That is how I remember Tilberthwaite Gill in the days before the war. It hurts me to see it now; the aids to progress up the gill have gone, and with their going has gone also the romantic appeal.

Tilberthwaite Gill

Crinkle Crags

2816 ft

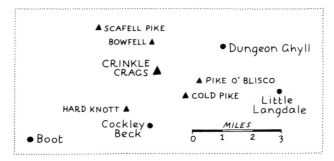

BOWFELL'S COMPANION AT THE head of Great Langdale was given the name of Crinkle Crags by the dalesfolk of that valley because of the succession of abrupt undulations on its long summit ridge. Seen from a distance these seem minor and of little consequence but on closer acquaintance are found to be not merely crinkly but exceedingly rough with a covering of boulders that would be difficult to negotiate were it not for a stony track trodden by the boots of countless walkers. Even so, this track bypasses three of the five distinct summits to avoid unfriendly conditions underfoot although it visits the two other tops where the terrain is more amenable. It is difficult for a layman to understand why the mountain is littered by boulders in such unbroken profusion and even a trained geologist must have doubts. Normally accumulations of rocky debris are found at the base of cliffs from which they have fallen, but that is not the explanation here where they occupy the highest ground; it is inconceivable that there was once a super-structure of crags throughout the length of the ridge that has now disintegrated. No, this carpet of stones has lain undisturbed through the ages since the land was formed by violent eruptions of natural forces.

The presence of so extensive a field of boulders, however, should not be a deterrent to active walkers, the traverse of the ridge being amongst the grandest mountain walks in Lakeland and strenuous effort will be recompensed by superlative views. Timid walkers will be less happy and may find the mountain hostile but should attempt it: other mountains are climbed and forgotten but Crinkle Crags will always be remembered.

Topographically, Crinkle Crags is an immense barrier with rugged ramifications descending to Great Langdale, Eskdale and the valley of the Duddon. The Langdale flank is buttressed by formidable cliffs denying access to the ridge above, the Eskdale side is a steep and rocky labyrinth offering no invitations, and its roots in the Duddon Valley support a fellside of unremitting steepness. No Lakeland mountain has a more impressive surround of natural defences. The main watercourses draining the mountain are Crinkle Gill, descending from a waste of scree in a ravine of cascades and waterslides to Oxendale, a branch of Great Langdale; Rest Gill and Swinsty Gill, debouching into Lingcove Beck in Eskdale, and the River Duddon and Mosedale Beck which form the southern and western boundaries.

Opposite Crinkle Crags from Crinkle Gill

ASCENTS

The usual routes of ascent, and the simplest, are from Wrynose Pass which carries a motor road, and from Great Langdale by way of Bowfell's Band and Three Tarns or, alternatively, by a circuitous route by Red Tarn.

Other routes described are pathless, totally unfrequented and remote from help in case of accident: they offer a challenge to adventurous spirits not less than two in number, or experienced solitary walkers.

FROM WRYNOSE PASS

Now that everybody seems to own a car, Wrynose Pass has become a popular springboard for the ascent, saving motorists a thousand feet of climbing. A path leaves the now obsolete Three Shire Stone for Red Tarn, there turning up a grassy slope to round Great Knott and so reach the first Crinkle. This approach is unexciting but, by making a detour from the path to the edge of Great Knott and looking down one of its gullies, a slender pinnacle of rock standing in isolation will be seen. Not many walkers know of this oddity but the Victorian pioneers did and named it Gladstone's Finger after their current hero.

Gladstone's Finger

FROM GREAT LANGDALE

For the minority who have no cars but arrive by foot or bus, the usual practice is to climb The Band on Bowfell to Three Tarns, there turning left along a path rounding Shelter Crags. Suddenly an assembly of Crinkles in close company is revealed directly ahead.

The alternative path climbs out of Oxendale to reach Red Tarn and there joins the route from Wrynose Pass.

CRINKLE GILL

This is no route for the squeamish. Without the help of a path, Crinkle Gill is followed up to its source in a waste of scree which must then be laboriously ascended to the gap of Mickledoor on the skyline between the two highest Crinkles.

FROM ESKDALE

The usual route of ascent from Eskdale, with the advantage of paths all the way, climbs to Three Tarns from Lingcove Beck and there turns right along the side of Shelter Crags to encounter the Crinkles at close range.

Rest Gill   *Crinkle Crags from Stonesty Pike*

There are, however, two alternatives, neither blessed with a path nor suitable for novice fellwalkers. The key to the first of these is Swinsty Gill which comes down the western slope of the Crinkles to join Lingcove Beck at the point where the side valley of Mosedale opens on the right. Swinsty Gill exploits a remarkable weakness in the mountain's defences, which relent here to admit a sheep pasture of rising grass. The gill is followed up its source in Adam-a-Cove, taking the left branch when it forks and so reaching the summit ridge. There are various rock outcroppings on the way but no difficulties underfoot. This is the only route by which the top of the mountain can be reached on grass throughout.

The second alternative is completely different in texture and character. It is initially a desperate scramble up the rocky canyon of Rest Gill which cuts across the path to Three Tarns and can be followed up from this point through a maze of rocks where every step has to be planned. Walking becomes easier when you can walk beside the stream on the way to its source. This route needs care but has two merits: it makes a beeline for the highest of the Crinkles and is a sure guide to the top in misty conditions.

FROM COCKLEY BECK IN THE DUDDON VALLEY

Much the easiest way from Cockley Beck is offered by the side valley of Mosedale where Swinsty Gill at its far end not only points the way but also acts as companion.

Much the hardest way is to tackle the steep slope above the intake wall, a route that shows little compassion for the climber until the 2000 ft contour is gained, when the way forward, after negotiating the outcrops of Little Stand and Stonesty Pike, is by comparison a simple stroll across an extensive plateau to join the path coming up from Red Tarn. This route becomes interesting after the initial hard labour, but the terrain is confusing in mist and should not then be attempted.

THE TRAVERSE OF CRINKLES

The measure of enjoyment derived from a traverse of Crinkle Crags from end to end depends on individual opinion. To a seasoned fellwalker it is sheer delight, often to be repeated; to a timid rambler it may well be an ordeal from which he is relieved to escape never to return.

The walking is abnormally rough throughout but within the capabilities of an active walker properly shod. Fine situations, beautiful and dramatic views and a constantly changing scene give a classic quality to this short journey.

The highest Crinkle is Long Top. Only one other of the five distinct Crinkles has a name, and it is usual to number them as they are met on the approach from Red Tarn, i.e. from south to north.

The first Crinkle is out of character; it has a level top so progress is easy amongst scattered rocks with a sensational view down into the profound abyss of Great Cove. At the end there is a short descent to a grassy saddle beyond which rises the second Crinkle, Long Top, the summit being most easily reached by walking left and ascending an open passage that leads directly to the top cairn. This route is preferred to the more obvious scree gully slanting upwards where the way is blocked by a huge chockstone jammed between the gully walls. This obstacle is the Bad Step, once considered impassable but I am told that it can now be bypassed via a tunnel scraped behind the chockstone.

Long Top and the Third Crinkle

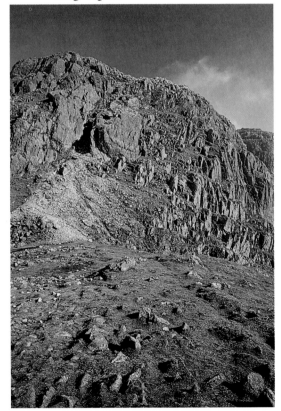

Tarn on Shelter Crags

Mickledoor and the Second Crinkle

From the summit of Long Top the remaining Crinkles are in view and a stony path goes down towards them with no awareness of the nearby crags that fall away in tiers into Great Cove; indeed, the upper part of Long Top has no threats and the few patches of grass make it a pleasant place for a picnic. It is even pleasanter if a tiny spring of water can be located amongst the upper rocks near the descending path: however, this fount of refreshment, the highest in Lakeland, is unreliable and often dry.

A short descent leads to a pronounced gap in the ridge, Mickledoor, from which a vast screeshoot falls into Great Cove between confining cliffs.

Immediately beyond Mickledoor rises the third Crinkle, and it is a pity that the path continues its downward trend and bypasses the summit. This omission is and should be remedied by a scramble up to its cairn for the superb view of Great Langdale seen from there.

Leaving Mickledoor the path slants down across the sides of the fourth and fifth Crinkles, bypassing their summits by an increasing margin as it descends. It is vastly more comfortable to walk upon than the boulders alongside which extend upwards to the skyline and are a persuasive deterrent to visits to their highest points. I am indeed sorry to have to ask Derry to toil up these hostile rocks with his camera and tripod to get pictures of the ultimate inches of the two Crinkles – the accompanying photographs prove that he not only did so but survived.

After passing the last Crinkle, which has the name of Gunson Knott, level and less stony ground is reached above a tremendous chasm on the right and the path, now more respectable, contours around the side of Shelter Crags on its final stage to Three Tarns. From this path there is a splendid retrospect of the Crinkles, standing in fine array and seeming to walkers of imagination to be saluting farewell; or, to those doing the traverse from the Three Tarns, a rather unfriendly welcome.

The sprawling top of Shelter Crags is rarely visited but is a notable viewpoint from which to appraise the Links of Bowfell. Easy slopes go down to Three Tarns, the path passing near a charming rock-girt pool, a glittering gem to crown a successful traverse of Crinkle Crags.

THE SUMMIT: 2816 FT

There are few places on the summit ridge of Crinkle Crags where one can sit in comfortable relaxation or walk freely without having to measure every step forward. Rather unexpectedly these simple pleasures are to be found on the highest summit of all, Long Top: there, although perched on a rocky plinth with fearsome crags only a few yards away there is no sense of danger.

Long Top is bulky, not as delicately sculptured as the others in the family, and has a shoulder of high ground extending towards Eskdale, hence the name. Descents must follow the path closely: there is no profit in personal deviations. A direct descent to Great Langdale is practicable only if prepared to do battle with the scree falling from Mickledoor. If proceeding south to the first Crinkle, the green rake descending from the summit avoids the Bad Step, and it should be noted that the grassy saddle between the two is the key to Adam-a-Cove and the easy slopes to Mosedale for Eskdale and the Duddon.

It is not only the opportunity to rest that halts visitors to Long Top. The all-round view abounds in detail and you should not hurry from here. Bowfell has pride of place amongst a crowd of mountains in the northern arc and the Scafell range is seen to perfection above the gulf of Upper Eskdale. Windermere and Esthwaite Water are the principal lakes in sight and a wide seascape in the far distance is marred only by the Sellafield power station.

Bowfell and the Scafell Range

COLD PIKE

The extensive southern slopes of Crinkle Crags decline gradually to an abrupt end on Wrynose Breast where they fall sharply to the infant River Duddon. Midway, their smooth passage is interrupted by the rocky ramparts of Cold Pike which cheekily apes its bigger neighbour by forming on a lesser scale a series of miniature crinkles, a jolly little set of knobs and pinnacles along a short summit ridge which is defended by a fringe of crags.

Left *Summit cairn, Long Top*
Below *The summit of Cold Pike*

Crinkle Crags from the summit of Cold Pike

Cold Pike is rarely visited, most walkers hereabouts having their sights fixed on its bigger neighbour, but it is easily reached by a deviation from the path rising from Red Tarn, or more directly by a beeline from any point on the path from Wrynose Pass to Red Tarn. In attempting the latter short cut one day in thick mist I proved the theory, which I had not previously believed to be true, that when unable to see ahead because of mist or darkness one tends to walk in circles. I had always prided myself on having an infallible sense of direction and had never before lost my way in mist but on this occasion my confidence was badly punctured. I left the path to Red Tarn and struck off across the trackless moor towards the hidden Cold Pike. After walking blindly for twenty minutes, I reached a distinct path and was amazed to be able to identify it as the one I had left earlier. I set off again and the same thing happened: after walking in what I thought to be a straight line I found myself back on the path again. Twice I had walked in a right-hand circle. I was shrouded in a blanket of mist, there was neither sun nor wind to give direction. After this galling experience I abandoned my intentions for the day, but it was a lesson I bore in mind for the future.

Dale Head

2473 ft

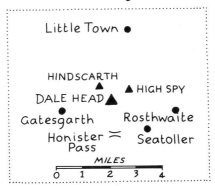

DALE HEAD IS NOT usually classed amongst the grandest of Lakeland's fells and is seldom the sole objective of an expedition: indeed, its modest altitude precludes its admission to the ranks of the greatest. Yet three good reasons merit its inclusion in this book: first, because it is the focal point of a semicircle of fells that together provide a horseshoe walk of infinite variety and interest; secondly, the summit commands a view of unsurpassed beauty, and thirdly, the climb up the north face of the mountain abounds in exciting and dramatic situations and, in the later stages, affords an absorbing test in route-finding in trackless terrain where maps are of little help.

Dale Head was obviously named by the early settlers in Newlands: it effectively terminates the upper reaches of that lovely valley, appearing as an immense barrier of forbidding cliffs in perpetual shadow, yet proving a good friend as a provider of the stream that nurtures the fertile pastures and meadows of Newlands and the mineral wealth that for centuries sustained the local economy. Copper mining was a major industry, while on the Honister flank huge slices were gouged out of the fellside by slate quarries; both enterprises are long abandoned, being fatal casualties in the march of progress. Today Dale Head is an industrial graveyard, a mouldering museum of relics of former activity, a place haunted by the ghosts of men who once laboured here. I am always saddened when I see ruins, especially those in lonely places where conditions must have been primitive. I find myself trying to imagine the folk who lived and worked there in happier days with no thought of the fate that was to befall them, of the heartbreak of their final departure, taking their memories and leaving behind so much to rot and decay. Ruins are the burial grounds of hopes and aspirations.

The southern boundary of Dale Head is formed by Honister Pass, the eastern is the minor eminence of High Scawdel, which falls sharply into Borrowdale and the western slopes merge at a high level with Hindscarth. In a land renowned for its profusion of lakes and tarns, Dale Head has the distinction of nursing in its lap the only sheet of water in the north-western fells which are singularly bereft of such amenities. This solitary exception is Dalehead Tarn.

Opposite *Dale Head from Hindscarth*

Honister from Dale Head

The summit of Dale Head is commonly reached as the midway point on the splendid round of the Newlands fells and approached either from High Spy by way of Dalehead Tarn or along the ridge from the neighbouring height of Hindscarth. Direct ascents may be made from the top of Honister Pass or by a choice of two routes from the valley of Newlands.

FROM HONISTER PASS

From a car parked at the quarry workings on Honister Pass, the climb is straightforward and simple, initially rather steep but becoming a mere stroll as the gradient eases; furthermore, it is foolproof even in misty conditions, an accompanying wire fence leading directly to the summit cairn, acting as an infallible guide. A disadvantage of this route is the absence of forward views until the top cairn is reached, exciting landscapes being seen only by looking back. One point of interest on the ascent occurs when the fence skirts the rim of the disused Yew Crag quarries.

Dale Head is the most easily attained major fell in Lakeland when the ascent is started from a car parked on Honister Pass; in fact, the amount of climbing is almost halved. Even if the walk starts from Seatoller, the extra effort is minimal.

FROM NEWLANDS VALLEY

Much more interesting is the ascent from the upper reaches of the Newlands Valley. The furthest point accessible by car is the hamlet of Little Town, an ambitious name for a tiny community which contains only a few houses and a farm, and from here a well-used track, originally serving the mines, leads directly to the foot of Dale Head between confining fells of considerable stature. After two miles with little gain in height, and beyond the prominent headland of Castlenook which thrusts aggressively into the floor of the valley, the cart track dwindles to a footpath: this climbs, inclining left below the beetling cliffs of Eel Crags, to a depression in the skyline ahead, and here, partly hidden by undulations, is Dalehead Tarn. From the tarn, a recently formed track mounts the steep breast of Dale Head and arrives at the summit. This is the usual route taken from the Newlands valley. When I first came this way before the war, as a raw novice illshod in rubber pumps, there was no track above the tarn and I was so exhausted on the steep final slope, having already walked from Keswick, that I was reduced to progressing on hands and knees. After a refreshing rest on the top, I was able to make my way down to Buttermere for a night's lodging.

The alternative route from the Newlands Valley is unfrequented, more adventurous and should be attempted only in clear weather. The higher stages of the climb have not the benefit of a path and are encompassed by intimidating crags.

Newlands Beck accompanies the walk from Little Town and, beyond Castlenook, where the path to Dalehead Tarn veers left and starts to climb, there was formerly a ford used on the way to or from the Dalehead Copper Mine. The ford is now unidentifiable and the old mine track the other side of the stream is indefinite but can be seen distinctly rising between the twin watercourses of Near Tongue Gill and Far Tongue Gill, both coming down from Hindscarth. The first-named is crossed low down and the track joined for the steady climb to the crossing of Far Tongue Gill which, when reached, is found to be not a twin at all; it emerges from a tremendous ravine far grander than anything the other can show. At this point the track advances in well-engineered zigzags to ease the passage of horses and sleds and is still in remarkably good condition after a century of disuse and neglect. The track ends at the copper mine, dramatically sited in the lee of the tremendous precipice of Gable Crag, the loneliness of the scene being emphasised by the derelict buildings. The problem of reaching the summit of the mountain, still far above, is solved by continuing up the rough grassy slope alongside the crags until abreast of their upper edge, then turning left along a rising shelf to its sudden end. Here the ground falls steeply to the hollow of Dalehead Tarn and a pleasant ridge then rises to the summit.

Gable Crag from the Dalehead Copper Mine

Castlenook and Dale Head

THE OLD MINES AT NEWLANDS

Looking today at Newlands, that vale of beauty and sanctuary of peace so sweetly representing the essence of rural tranquillity, it is difficult to conceive that for centuries it was a centre of mining activity, that the rich pastures and verdant fellsides concealed underground wealth. Yet for many generations men laboured there to extract precious ores of lead and copper, and even of silver and gold. All the workings are now closed and abandoned; there is silence where once there was animated effort and the scars of industry are slowly healing.

In the wider cultivated part of the valley, long fans of scree and spoil pour down from the defunct and once famous Barrow Mine, threatening the motor road below. The rubble is so dense that nature is having a hard task in trying to clothe the valley sides with vegetation and probably never will.

At Stonythwaite Bridge nearby, there are evidences of a former lead mine in the form of watercuts carved in the rocks alongside the stream bed and a level half-hidden and now defended by gorse bushes. Across the valley, on the side of Catbells above Little Town, are the decaying remains of the Yewthwaite Mine with unprotected shafts that can be lethal traps, as events have proved.

But the main industrial sites occur in the narrow upper reaches of the valley, once known as Dale Head Glen. Very prominent is the site of Castlenook Mine on a projecting headland. In its heyday this had a waterwheel, but now few traces remain. If any of the remaining shafts are explored, great care should be taken.

At the foot of Dale Head, just beyond the confluence of Far Tongue Gill and Newlands Beck, the ground is pitted by shafts and man-made water channels, one of which has mellowed into a charming rock pool. The Dalehead Copper Mine, halfway up the mountain and less easy to reach, is spectacularly sited. Small spoil-heaps near the ruined buildings contain stones with bright green veins of copper malachite.

Goldscope Mine, situated on a spur of Hindscarth, Scope End, is the most famous of all the industrial workings in the Newlands Valley. It was originally developed by German miners and was in operation for six centuries. Its fame is understandable since lead, copper, silver and gold were all mined here. Fearsome levels tunnel into the fellside and are extremely dangerous.

THE SUMMIT: 2473 FT

The summit of Dale Head is a simple mound with a magnificent cairn of slate built by a professional craftsman, a work of art that should be revered as much as a monument in a churchyard. Geologists report that there is a fusion hereabouts of Skiddaw slate and the volcanic rock of central Lakeland, but it needs a trained eye to detect the point of convergence. Slopes fall away gently to south, west and east, but northwards are precipitous crags, and descent in this direction is not advised unless already familiar with the terrain.

The views are excellent and well balanced in all directions, but may disappoint visitors whose eyes search first for lakes and tarns since the panorama is almost exclusively of mountains and fells. The Scafells and Great Gable are compelling attractions in the south, but best of all is the lovely prospect of Newlands, seen aerially as it fades into the distance, heading due north to be halted by Skiddaw. This view is a gem.

The summit cairn, Dale Head

Catbells and Derwentwater from Maiden Moor

THE NEWLANDS HORSESHOE

Walks around the ridges enclosing a valley, making a complete circuit of the surrounding fells, are becoming increasingly popular in Lakeland: they offer excellent expeditions at a high level with the comfort of a path underfoot, reveal a succession of changing views, and survey, as from an aeroplane, every aspect of the valley below. They have also the decided advantage, in these days when it is usual to begin from a parked car, of returning a walker to his starting point. These circuits of the high ground around the heads of valleys are known as horseshoe walks.

The traverse of the fells on either side of Newlands is a joyful exercise of sustained exhilaration with views both beautiful and dramatic every step of the way. Nowhere is the walking difficult; there are no hazards and a steady pace can be maintained along the tops. I rank the Newlands Horseshoe among the best.

A convenient starting point is Hawes End on the west shore of Derwentwater, and the first objective is Catbells, the name probably a corruption of Cat Bields, a shelter for wild cats. Catbells is very popular with visitors to Keswick and a favourite for families, but the crowds do not persist beyond the summit. Here a slight depression is crossed and a rising path followed to the top of Maiden Moor; this section has wonderful views of Derwentwater and the surrounding landscape.

The path crosses to the Newlands edge of Maiden Moor and gives sensational glimpses of that valley. After a level half-mile it ascends to the top of High Spy, perched above an impressive wall of crags overlooking the head of Newlands and most effectively barring descents in that direction: these are Eel Crags, a haunt of rock-climbers. The path skirts the edge of the cliffs as it descends easily to the depression of Rigg Head, where Dalehead Tarn is the key to the steep slope leading up to the summit of Dale Head which is the halfway point of the horseshoe.

Eel Crags from Dale Head Below *Summit cairn on High Spy*

From the top of Dale Head a path leads west alongside the few surviving posts of an old fence and descends gradually to a narrow depression beyond which the fence is left for a beeline trek to the summit of Hindscarth in the north. An untidy pile of stones marks the highest, but of more interest is a cairn and wall shelter a short distance further: this is indicated on Ordnance maps as an antiquity and stands on the edge of a steep declivity into the next valley, Littledale.

Continuing due north, a descending ridge between unseen cliffs ends in a delightful spur of dense heather, a charming path following the crest to its termination at Scope End. This is pierced by the tunnels of the Goldscope Mine, a place of historic interest that was worked from the fourteenth century and considered the most important mine in the district until its closure a hundred years ago. From this point on the last lap of the journey, the whole route of the horseshoe can be seen. An easy descent to the attractive Newlands Church completes a memorable day.

Eel Crag

2749 ft

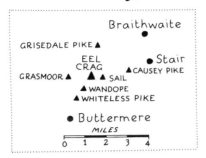

THE ORDNANCE SURVEY PERSISTS in naming this mountain Crag Hill, and although it must be assumed that they are correct in doing so, their choice of name has never been generally accepted, Eel Crag being preferred by guidebook writers and walkers. Jenkinson's guidebook, written in the middle of last century, and Baddeley's more recent one both described it as Eel Crag without mention of Crag Hill as an option and it is as Eel Crag that the mountain is popularly known. Even this is a misnomer however, since the cliffs of the undisputed Eel Crag are half a mile distant from the summit and overlook Coledale Hause.

The mountain is best viewed from Coledale where it dominates the head of the valley. It also presents a tremendous broadside to the deep trench of Sail Beck, but apart from these aspects it lacks distinction of outline and despite its impressive bulk does not have the magnetic appeal of other more shapely heights in Lakeland. Nevertheless, it is of strategic importance geographically as the hub of a group of fells, a watershed of streams draining both north and south, although all are within the gathering grounds of the River Derwent. It is buttressed by ascending ridges from Newlands and Buttermere, the full traverse giving a splendid walk between the two valleys.

The great feature of the mountain is the north-east flank, steeply descending in a wild confusion of crags and outcrops and runs of scree that repel exploration; the south face, too, is defended by a line of cliffs and only westwards is there a simple slope of easy gradient. In the south, between Eel Crag and the neighbouring height of Wandope, is a vast hollow of special interest, a perfect example of a hanging valley to which the contours of the Ordnance maps do not do justice: this is Addacomb Hole where a great scoop gouged out of the fellside is halted midway on its fall to Sail Beck.

Eel Crag is the pivot of the north-western fells and is the greatest influence in the surrounding landscape but is not the highest point, that honour going to Grasmoor, a compelling and more readily identifiable object only a mile away in the west and linked by an ascending ridge, but Grasmoor has no subservient satellites and it is to Eel Crag that the fells of Whiteless Pike, Wandope, Sail and Causey Pike have an affinity. Eel Crag is the head of a family; Grasmoor is without kin.

Eel Crag has escaped the attention of miners and quarrymen and remains as primeval and untamed as when fashioned long ages ago but it commands an oversight of two industrial enterprises of unusual interest: the long-established barytes mine at Force Crag in Coledale, intermittently worked, and the only cobalt mine in the district, disused and forgotten, on the side of Scar Crags.

Opposite *Eel Crag from Coledale Hause*

Gasgale Gill

ASCENTS

Eel Crag does not invite direct ascents from valley levei, the approaches to the summit being guarded by rough and inhospitable slopes and encompassed by supporting heights. These defences, however, can be breached at a few points of weakness, the orthodox and usual route being along Coledale, the later stages of the climb being made circuitous by impending crags. More straightforward but rougher underfoot is a path alongside Gasgale Gill from Lanthwaite. The finest way of reaching the top, however, is along the ridge from Causey Pike, passing over three intermediate summits; the ridge from Whiteless Pike comes a good second.

FROM THE WEST

There is no alternative to Gasgale Gill, a wild ravine between Whiteside and Grasmoor entered through rocky portals. It has the advantage of a path leading to Coledale Hause where the final slope of Eel Crag appears immediately ahead in a covering of loose scree at a steep angle; this is not easy to surmount but gives access to an exciting traverse along the edge of the north-eastern cliffs to the summit cairn.

FROM THE SOUTH-WEST

The Ordnance map suggests Rannerdale Beck as a possible line of ascent and this stream has the merit of pointing the way directly to the summit with no fear of straying even in the thickest mist but the route has so many disadvantages that it cannot be recommended: it is rough, pathless, without views and, being in a deep cutting between the steep fellsides of Grasmoor and Whiteless Pike, is claustrophobic. There is a pretty waterfall near the start above the intake wall but, this apart, there is no beauty in the constricted scene and nothing worthy of a photograph.

FROM THE SOUTH

Much the best approach to Eel Crag from the Buttermere valley first climbs the grassy slopes of Whiteless Pike on a popular path to its neat top, enjoying beautiful views throughout, and thence continues along a narrow ridge to Thirdgillhead Man. From here a simple detour to Wandope may be made before ascending the easy slope directly ahead to Eel Crag's summit cairn. This route is pleasant, mildly exciting, with grass underfoot most of the way and avoids the worst of the screes that litter the sides of the crag.

FROM BRAITHWAITE

The village of Braithwaite is the usual starting point for the ascent of Eel Crag, a straight two-mile mine road leading into the heart of a compact group of high fells with the objective clearly seen ahead. The route forks left before reaching Force Crag mines crossing Coledale Beck and rising, still on a distinct track, to bypass the mine workings and arrive at Coledale Hause. Here a sharp turn left up a steep and tedious ladder of unstable scree leads to the exciting summit ridge and the highest cairn.

A spice of adventure can be introduced into the walk, and a more direct ascent achieved, by following upwards the course of a streamlet below the first tier of crags on the mountain until a breach admits to a shelf above; this rises to the right and avoids the worst of the scree above the Hause. Or, better still, get a taste of real mountaineering by scrambling up the side of the buttress above the breach, a test in route-finding, to emerge amid thrilling rock scenery on the summit ridge with the highest point within easy reach.

Eel Crag from Coledale

THE EAST RIDGE

Eel Crag has its eastern roots in Newlands and a well-defined ridge ascends there from the village of Stair, its gradual rise being interrupted by three minor heights classed as separate fells but linked together at a high level to provide a fellwalk of high quality and increasing interest. This is the finest approach to Eel Crag.

A good path slants upwards aiming for Causey Pike, identifiable by the rocky knob of its summit, the final stage of the ascent being steep and the last few yards a rough scramble to the cairn. Here tired legs can be rested while eyes can feast on a lovely view of the Derwentwater countryside and a sensational one into the depths of Rigg Beck far below. The top of Causey Pike, a narrow crest with a succession of bumps, is delightful and is followed by a steady rise to the summit of Scar Crags, so named after a long line of cliffs alongside the path. A short descent then leads to a depression crossed by Sail Pass.

This point can be reached with less effort but less pleasure by using the old mine road from Stoneycroft, near Stair, made originally to serve the cobalt mine a short distance from Sail Pass: this alternative route, after an initial incline to the grassy plateau of High Moss, turns up to the disused mine, of which little remains, and the pass is then only a short distance further. The next objective is Sail, a fell lacking character and interest, and reached by an easy climb. Beyond is a narrow rocky ridge, which provides excitement on the final rise to the summit of Eel Crag, arriving there with the top cairn close at hand.

The summit of Eel Crag

The view southwards

THE SUMMIT: 2749 FT

The highest point is distinguished by an Ordnance Survey column, but is otherwise unpretentious, being flat and littered with slate fragments. It is a place to halt and admire a diverse panorama but bear in mind that wandering around the top is severely restricted by cliffs immediately east and south.

The view is almost exclusively of mountains and fells, these forming the horizon in all directions; the southern skyline is particularly impressive. Lakes and tarns are not much in evidence and it is disappointing to find the nearby lakes of Buttermere and Crummock Water concealed from sight by intervening fells.

Descent from the summit needs care, especially in bad weather conditions. If aiming for Coledale Hause and its safe path, it is preferable to go down west to the headwaters of Gasgale Gill and follow the stream down to the Hause, thus avoiding the slopes of scree on the direct descent; if bound for Newlands, the east ridge can be left at Sail Pass in favour of the mine road to Stoneycroft. For Buttermere, the landmark to head for is the massive cairn on Thirdgillhead Man, which marks the direction to the path over Whiteless Pike.

Fairfield

2863 ft

FAIRFIELD, LONG REGARDED AS rather a dull mountain lacking in interest and excitement, contributed much to the resurging interest in fellwalking which took place after the war. Since then, it has grown in status in the minds of fellwalkers, and really came into its own when it was recognised as the apex and central point of a circular walk at a high level in which no fewer than eight separate summits could be reached in the course of a day's expedition.

Fairfield stands at the meeting place of two parallel ridges enclosing a deep valley. The whole walk as seen on a map forms a horseshoe in plan, with the decided advantage for the many who now walk from parked cars, of returning the walker to his starting point.

Today the Fairfield Horseshoe is a classic test of a fellwalker's ability and is one of the most favoured walks in Lakeland: there are few days in the year when the summit cairn on Fairfield does not have visitors, and on most days it has many.

Rather to be regretted is the adoption of the Horseshoe as a racecourse for fellrunners racing against the clock: records have been established and broken. I admire and envy the energy of those who can travel over rough mountain terrain at high speed but find it difficult to imagine the pleasure they derive from doing so. Mountains are not race tracks, should not become places of competition: they have so much to offer, not only in healthy exercise but in the study of plant and animal life, the rock formations, the way the land has been shaped, and the superlative views, all of which should be enjoyed at leisure with many halts. The Fairfield Horseshoe deserves eight hours, not two.

The Horseshoe walk, however, does not yield a full appreciation of the mountain, of the massive build up from the surrounding valleys, and in fact skirts unseen the most impressive and dramatic features. Fairfield is much more than a time-check on a felltop marathon.

Opposite *Fairfield from Deepdale*

65

Fairfield is a sprawling maze of high ground with no grace of outline and a summit so lacking in immediate interest that only the distant views encourage a leisurely halt. The extensive top is almost level for half a mile, easy to walk upon but without incident.

The mountain is connected to two neighbouring heights, Hart Crag east and Great Rigg south, with little loss of altitude and only in the south-east is there a free fall to a valley: this, the only major valley in Lakeland without an official name, is commonly and conveniently referred to as Rydale. To the west there is also an uninterrupted drop of a thousand feet to Grisedale Hause. Otherwise, Fairfield's roots are cramped and confined by its satellites.

It is the north flank that gives Fairfield distinction. In complete contrast to its bland appearance in other directions, a series of rocky buttresses and screeshoots plunge suddenly from the edge of the summit plateau into the head of Deepdale with startling ferocity: it is a dramatic scene that escapes attention on the southern and western approaches. On this side too is a narrow ridge, the most exciting of all, that drops sharply to Deepdale Hause and gives spectacular views of the northern face. This side of the mountain is grim indeed: it is as though Fairfield, so bland and benign otherwise, here had had a fit of bad temper. The eastern boundary overlooking Link Cove is also defended by a line of cliffs culminating in the tremendous headland of Greenhow End. To appreciate the majesty of Fairfield, the approach to it should be made along the valley of Deepdale.

ASCENTS

Fairfield is so closely supported by other fells that it does not lend itself easily to direct ascents avoiding intermediate heights – the top usually being reached by way of the southern ridges forming the horseshoe. Maps suggest a straightforward route, almost a beeline, that starts from Rydal village on a path that follows the course of Rydal Beck for four miles to Rydal Head and there tackling the steep slopes ahead, skirting Black Crag and minor outcrops to emerge on the summit plateau. This route, although as straight as a ruler, has never found favour, the valley becoming constricted and the final climb pathless and uninviting. Much more frequented is a route that goes up from Grasmere to Grisedale Hause and there turns right in the company of a wall that points the way to the top. For walkers based in the Patterdale area, the route along Deepdale, which rounds the base of St. Sunday Crag and persists to the head of the valley at Deepdale Hause, there turning left up the ridge of Cofa Pike to the summit, is unquestionably the finest direct way, the last mile being in scenes of wild grandeur below the ramparts of the mountain.

Walkers who are not averse to crossing other summits on the way to Fairfield will approach it along one or other of the southern ridges, but again it is those coming from Patterdale who have the opportunity of making the most thrilling ascent of all: this climbs through Glenamara Park to a splendid path along the side of Birks leading to the upper slopes of St. Sunday Crag, from the top of which an easy descent follows to Deepdale Hause and a final steep scramble over Cofa Pike to Fairfield's summit. Just before reaching the highest cairn on St. Sunday Crag, a cluster of embedded rock flakes makes an interesting foreground to a perfect full-length view of Ullswater, a classic composition of lake and mountains in harmonious relationship, a gem for the camera.

Opposite *Ullswater from St Sunday Crag*

THE SUMMIT: 2863 FT

Too many cairns on a mountain top can be more misleading than too few and this is well demonstrated on Fairfield. The summit cairn, a large and untidy heap of stones, is not in doubt but there is a rash of others all around, some of them serving the useful purpose of indicating the path, others merely causing confusion in mist; a few are even dangerously perched on the edge of the northern cliffs, presumably as warning. In clear weather there are no problems of route selection; the broad top is a simple promenade on trodden paths.

Descents are invariably made along one of the southern ridges, the easiest being over Great Rigg and Nab Scar to Rydal. In bad conditions, the descent to Grisedale Hause is the best line of escape, there joining the Grasmere-Patterdale path. Deepdale has no merit in such conditions.

The summit cairn

The top of Fairfield is a watershed: south-flowing streams enter Windermere on their passage to Morecambe Bay, those flowing north find their way into Ullswater for an ultimate destiny in the Solway Firth.

Fairfield's superior altitude is reflected in the uninterrupted panorama in all points of the compass, a far-reaching view almost exclusively of mountains and fells extending to distant horizons. Disappointingly, the nearby lakes and valleys are hidden by the wide spread of the flat top. The grandest feature of the mountain, often unnoticed by visitors to the summit, is best seen by descending the short ridge to Cofa Pike where the northern cliffs, abruptly terminated by Greenhow End, are displayed in profile, a most impressive scene.

The High Bakestones near Dove Crag

High Pike from the summit of Low Pike

THE FAIRFIELD HORSESHOE

The Fairfield Horseshoe has become established as a favourite expedition for fellwalkers; the eleven-mile journey at a high level presents a challenge few can resist. The walk may be done in either direction, the least arduous in terms of gradient being anti-clockwise and is generally preferred.

Starting from Ambleside, it is usual to take the lovely lane to High Sweden Bridge, there slanting upwards across the fellside of Low Pike, bypassing the summit to reach the ridge at midpoint. But this is cheating. The purist determined to do the whole horseshoe and no short cuts will commence at the roots of the ridge near Low Sweden Bridge and follow it upwards alongside a wall to the rocky top of Low Pike, then descending to a depression below High Pike where the alternative route via High Sweden Bridge joins in.

A steady and uneventful climb leads to the top of High Pike. Do spend some time studying the accompanying wall which is an object lesson in the art of drystone walling and testimony to the skill of the forgotten men who built it nearly 200 years ago. The stones are laid in horizontal courses despite the steepness of the ground.

Dovedale from Dove Crag

Beyond High Pike, the wall begins to crumble but points the way to the next summit, Dove Crag, along an easy incline, the route there trending north-west.

Visitors arriving on the summit of Dove Crag may well wonder about the name since there is no crag in sight along the top of the fell which is relatively smooth and without even minor undulations. The crag, although unseen from the summit, removes all doubts of its existence if a five-minute detour is made down the easy northern slope to the edge of a fearful precipice, the ground collapsing suddenly and without warning in a vertical and overhanging cliff: this is the most severe climbing ground in the eastern fells. The edge should be approached gingerly; it is not protected by a fence and a step too many will bring the horseshoe walk to an abrupt and fatal conclusion.

Dove Crag, from which the fell is named, is awesome and even frightening, the sort of place that inspires nightmares, and its abrupt edge, to the left of the great gully that splits it asunder, has more than a spice of danger. However, before fleeing back to the safety of the ridge, the view forward over the vast abyss directly below deserves detailed study from a secure stance: in peaceful contrast to the starkness of the viewpoint, the lovely valley of Dovedale is seen threading its way through a rugged landscape to the fields of Hartsop.

The Step

The ridge declines to a depression with the next objective, Hart Crag, rising ahead, and the summit of this rocky height is attained after a sharp climb. Look back and you will see Dove Crag in profile. Hart Crag commands a full length view of Rydale to the left and overlooks Link Cove on the right. The path goes down to a pronounced gap in the ridge known as The Step and here a narrow crest links Hart Crag and Fairfield in surroundings of primeval desolation. In the event of the onset of bad weather, The Step is the best place to leave the ridge, a steep slope leading left down to Rydal Head and a safe return to base.

Across The Step, the path climbs to the broad top of Fairfield and leads unerringly to the summit cairn or, alternatively and more excitingly, the edge of the northern cliffs may be followed on a parallel course. The cairn marks the turning point of the walk and the end of hard work; reaching it is an occasion for celebration. Before starting the homeward trek, however, a short detour to Cofa Pike is recommended for the view of the northern facade of the mountain.

Continuing the horseshoe, the next summit, Great Rigg, is reached along a gentle descending slope heading due south, followed by a short rise. From whatever direction seen, Great Rigg appears as a symmetrical dome and it is a surprise to find that the top is a level sward of excellent turf, good enough and large enough to accommodate a cricket match.

Fairfield from Loughrigg Fell

From Great Rigg, a spur branches to the right and offers a quick descent to Grasmere by way of Stone Arthur, while the horseshoe walk persists due south, descending to pass over the double top of Heron Pike before declining to the last summit, Nab Scar. Here further progress forward is ruled out by the steepness and cragginess of its south slope overlooking Rydal Water, of which it has a lovely bird's-eye view. Now the path inclines left and descends abruptly and unpleasantly, becoming badly eroded by heavy foot-traffic: rough steps have been constructed here to induce walkers not to stray on the verges and so cause further unsightly damage.

Erosion of mountain paths is a growing problem in Lakeland and should not have to happen. It is caused by clumsy and careless walkers: those who travel at speed, especially in descent, loosening and scattering the surface of paths into runs of scree, and by those parties who travel abreast to maintain conversations and in so doing trample upon and uproot the verges. Mountain paths should be walked in single file and preferably in silence; noisy chatter is out of place in the mountains.

The slope gradually eases, trees are a welcome sight after a day spent on barren uplands, and Rydal is reached after a pleasant downhill stroll.

Tired legs and happy faces are the after-effects of this walk and the final ritual is the sending of postcards home announcing the conquest of the Fairfield Horseshoe.

Glaramara

2560 ft

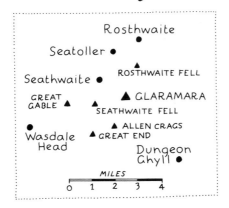

GLARAMARA IS MORE THAN a pretty name. It is a mountain of distinction, not amongst the highest or more exciting in Lakeland and lacking a shapely outline, yet having so many features of interest that fellwalkers always look forward to a visit with eager anticipation. There is never a dull moment on Glaramara.

There is nothing compelling about the appearance of the mountain which rises steeply as a wedge of rough upland springing from the verdant pastures at the head of Borrowdale. Its appeal lies in the delightful traverse of the summit ridge, the unsurpassed views and its dominant role in the Borrowdale scene as the guardian of the upper reaches of that loveliest of valleys.

Glaramara may be said to terminate the massive Scafell range in the north, bringing to an end the high ground that leaves Scafell Pike, collapses midway in the cliffs of Great End and then recovers height in Allen Crags and from there maintains a lofty elevation along the top of Glaramara before finally descending, rugged aggression spent, to the pastoral peace of cultivated fields and woodlands where man takes over from nature. The boundaries of Glaramara are clearly defined by Langstrath Beck in the east and Grains Gill and the River Derwent in the west, their waters meeting as the slopes decline to valley level. The main watercourse, coming directly off the mountain is Comb Gill which flows due north to join the Derwent after passing through a wide hollow notable for having the greatest crag on the mountain and the only natural caves in Lakeland. On the summit ridge is a necklace of small tarns, enchanting pools that halt the steps of every walker on the path alongside, one in particular occupying a rocky basin and making a picture so endearing that I have long considered it the most charming tarn in the district.

Glaramara is of simple construction with only one offshoot from the main spine; this branches off at Comb Head to form Rosthwaite Fell, an upland of much fascination, a labyrinth of tors and hollows that has inherited the charms of the valley around its base.

Opposite *Glaramara from Castle Crag*

ASCENTS

The only convenient direct ascent of Glaramara leaves the Borrowdale road at Mountain View, near Seatoller, passes through the pleasant woodland alongside Comb Gill and, when clear of trees, follows a rising path over Thornythwaite Fell to the summit. This route, however, has the disadvantage of having the best views behind and is better reserved for descent.

Much the finest approach is from the south, traversing the mountain from end to end. This entails a preliminary climb to the wall shelter at the top of the Langdale–Wasdale pedestrian highway, commonly but wrongly called Esk Hause; from Borrowdale this well-known landmark can be reached by way of Grains Gill. The wall shelter stands at an altitude of almost 2400 feet and therefore the hardest part of the climb has already been accomplished when it is reached: from this point little further effort is needed to arrive at the summit. The way lies over Allen Crags to a depression and a cluster of small tarns in an attractive setting, after which a delightful path threads through rough surroundings to the summit cairn.

The descent is usually made to Borrowdale by passing over the declining ridge of Thornythwaite Fell, a most enjoyable way down with entrancing views of the valley directly ahead to Derwentwater and the Skiddaw group. Walkers bound for Langdale or Wasdale have no option but to retrace their steps to the wall shelter.

Left *The Lincomb Tarn*
Below *Borrowdale from Bessyboot*

The Summit: 2560 ft

Glaramara has two summits close together, almost twins, both having cairns perched on rocky outcrops and defended by low crags, both being of similar appearance and elevation; the most northerly is recognised as the summit proper. The ridge path passes between them.

They stand at the extremity of the long and fairly level traverse from the tarns below Allen Crags, and the ground then commences an unbroken decline towards Borrowdale.

From every part of the top of Glaramara the views are outstanding. The Langdale Pikes have an unfamiliar outline, appearing as minor pinnacles at the end of a lofty hinterland across Langstrath. The southern arc is crowded with range after range of mountains all splendidly displayed and forming a serrated skyline: the Coniston Fells, the Crinkles and Bowfell groups, Great End hiding the Scafells and, round to the west and north, Great Gable is a dominant object across Sty Head, followed by Pillar, the High Stile ridge, Grasmoor and the north-western fells. Due north is the only lake to be seen, Derwentwater, with Skiddaw behind and Blencathra near. The eastern horizon is closed by the long Helvellyn range. There are glimpses of the Irish Sea and the West Cumbria coast. All in all, a wonderfully detailed panorama.

Right *Glaramara's main summit*
Below *Great Gable and Pillar from Glaramara*

Stanger Gill

Tarn at Leaves

ROSTHWAITE FELL

Glaramara has few complications, having no beguiling side ridges to tempt walkers astray nor confusing undulations or recesses. It is a straightforward and honest mountain with no intention of creating or causing difficulties in route finding.

However, at Comb Head, just north of the main summit and at the top of Comb Gill, a connection is made with another area of high ground too distinguished in character to be termed a branch of Glaramara and fully deserving its individual name of Rosthwaite Fell. This is a delightful field of exploration and well worth a separate half-day expedition. It is steep-sided and pathless, ruling out direct access everywhere and only from the Stonethwaite valley can the top be reached without discomfort; happily this route is accompanied by scenes and views of natural beauty and a spice of excitement as it climbs through a ravine enclosed by crags.

The key to the ascent is Stanger Gill and a simple instruction would be to follow the stream upwards to its source, but some detail is merited.

Stanger Gill comes steeply down the northern slope to join Stonethwaite Beck, the climb being started from the lane which leads beyond the hamlet of Stonethwaite. A path leads up through a scattering of trees, aiming for a great notch in the skyline formed by the passage of the gill between the cliffs of Bull Crag and Hanging Haystacks. Through this cleft, the top of the fell is reached in confusing terrain but the stream gives direction and its source in marshy ground is within shouting distance of the summit, which rejoices in the name of Bessyboot.

Bessyboot at 1807ft is regarded as the summit of Rosthwaite Fell although there are slightly higher elevations towards its link with Glaramara. It rises at the end of a series of rocky knobs on a declining spur, its neat and pleasant top being easily achieved by a breach in the low crags around it. The main interest lies in the view, which is unexpectedly comprehensive away from the bulk of Glaramara but disappointing because the surrounding valleys are obscured by the broad top of the fell.

Continuing north, the only sheet of water on the fell is reached at once: this is Tarn at Leaves, a pretty name for a rather dreary reality and no place for a picnic. Its issuing stream, let it be noted in bad weather, descends into mid-Langstrath, not Borrowdale.

Beyond Tarn at Leaves, the ground rises to the highlight of the fell, a place much more worthy of a picnic stop than the tarn. This is Rosthwaite Cam, an attractive turret of grey rock with a cairn perched aloft, a conspicuous tor that might well also stake a claim as the true summit of the fell.

An alternative to Stanger Gill as a route of descent may be made from this point by continuing to Comb Head and following Comb Gill down to the road to Borrowdale.

On the fellside below Rosthwaite Cam and overlooking Comb Gill are the Dovenest Crags and here a minor convulsion of nature has resulted in a rock slip that stripped the cliffs of huge slabs, these having come to rest in a great pile covering an interior cavity to which there are three entrances: these are the Doves Nest Caves. A scree path leads up the fellside to Doves Nest Caves. Explorers of the subterranean passages usually enter the South Cave and emerge higher at Attic Cave after a rock-climb made difficult by a total absence of daylight. Wise walkers will peep into the darkness but keep out. Apart from wedged chockstones in gullies, those at Doves Nest are the only natural caves in the district, the adits and levels found in quarries and mines being man-made. They are quite unlike the caves of the Craven underworld which are caused by the action of water on limestone; the rocks here are volcanic and impervious to water.

View to Borrowdale from Comb Head

Grasmoor

2791 ft

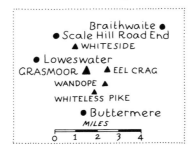

GRASMOOR IS THE GIANT of the north-western fells in terms of feet and inches but superior height alone is not always a measure of importance. As is the case here, Grasmoor plays a reluctant second fiddle to its lesser neighbour, Eel Crag. Grasmoor is rather out on a limb, away from the centre of topographical happenings, the role of pivot being assumed by Eel Crag which exercises an influence and overview of the surrounding terrain, is the culmination of ascending ridges, determines the direction of flow of its streams and generally acts as a father figure to the lesser fells in its immediate vicinity. Grasmoor has no such attributes: it stands alone, aloof, of massive proportions but with no supporting ridges, no subservient satellites, no family of its own and no close friends, and is unable to give its streams a choice of direction. Its one great appeal lies in the magnificent panorama afforded by its superior height.

Grasmoor excels, however, in its presentation to the Buttermere road at its base of a tremendous west face which soars nearly half a mile into the sky as a towering pyramid of intimidating aspect. No other mountain in Lakeland has so impressive an appearance from a public road. Beyond the grassy verges the ground steepens dramatically, becoming near-vertical as it leaps upwards and then narrows to a rocky apex above a savage downfall of scree, rocks and crags in a petrified avalanche of mountain debris. The face is split asunder by two sinister gullies where rock-climbers find limited sport but for walkers is quite unassailable and out of bounds. One look is sufficient to deter any thought of ascent, and significantly there are no foot-tracks leading even initially towards the sudden upsurge directly in front. It is remarkable that, although Grasmoor is very conveniently positioned for direct ascent, being alongside a road with ample car parking spaces, the challenge goes unheeded, the aspect of the mountain on this side being too daunting and formidable even to contemplate.

Nor are the two flanks any more promising. The north side overlooking Gasgale Gill is equally steep with scree runs falling from a top barrier of cliffs and continuing with little respite to Dove Crags, the gradients easing only as Coledale Hause is approached. The other side, facing south-east over the deep cutting of Rannerdale Beck, is a waste of scree at a high angle and totally uninviting.

The boundaries of Grasmoor are clearly defined by Gasgale Gill and Rannerdale Beck, both watercourses destined for the River Cocker, the Rannerdale stream first passing through Crummock Water. To add to its demerits, Grasmoor has no tarns to show to visitors but they will be more than compensated by the superlative views of the Buttermere lakes it commands.

Opposite *Grasmoor from the Buttermere road*

ASCENTS

There are few weaknesses in the structure of Grasmoor by which the summit may be attained and only one that permits an easy approach, the others being expensive in energy and physical discomfort. The west face must be ruled out entirely as impossibly steep and unsafe.

VIA COLEDALE HAUSE

The usual route, and much the simplest, is by way of Coledale Hause, reached by paths from Braithwaite or Lanthwaite after a considerable climb to almost 2000 feet. Here Gasgale Gill, now in its infancy, turns sharply south to its source in a hollow between Eel Crag and Grasmoor. An interesting feature at the bend in the stream is a man-made water cut, now dry, that originally diverted water across the hause to supply the mines at the head of Coledale. Gasgale Gill is followed up until the east ridge of Grasmoor offers an easy walk, gently rising and skirting the rim of Dove Crags and ending with a stroll on mossy turf to the summit.

Grasmoor from Lanthwaite Hill

Cinderdale Beck

VIA DOVE CRAGS

The Gasgale slopes of the mountain are excessively steep and unstable but at one point there is a breach in the long line of cliffs supporting the summit ridge, giving an opportunity for a pathless and unorthodox ascent. This occurs when the Gasgale path is below the semicircle of Dove Crags; the stream is forded and a long grass slope ascended to pass alongside the crags and emerge on the ridge. As the climb proceeds, a green hollow at the foot of the crags is revealed, a natural amphitheatre that looks fashioned to hold a tarn but surprisingly does not.

VIA LAD HOWS

Lad Hows is a minor protuberance above the Buttermere road and may be used as a springboard for an ascent that proves to be steep and stony and a torment for those who prefer to walk circumspectly. From Lad Hows, the route makes its way up an indefinite ridge, guided by a path that finally peters out in very rough terrain where a last undignified scramble brings the summit underfoot.

    The initial climb to Lad Hows (Ladhouse on old maps) is pleasant, the path to it from the road coming alongside Cinderdale Beck, a charming stream flowing in a series of waterfalls between banks of bracken and heather. It is a place often populated by motorists from parked cars at the roadside as a place for a picnic and an exercise for the legs.

Red Gill

VIA RED GILL

Walkers based in the Buttermere valley and wanting to climb Grasmoor but who do not take kindly to the idea of going the long way round by Gasgale Gill and Coledale Hause have an obvious alternative staring them in the face as they stand on the road near Cinderdale Beck. Coming directly down from the summit is the long white ribbon of Red Gill, a straight ladder of stones reached by crossing an open common alongside a descending stream and, beyond its source, entering upon the thousand-foot scree run of Red Gill. This is an arduous scramble over sliding stones from which a final escape may be made over rough ground and, still climbing steeply, up to the summit. Every step of this route is upwards without respite. It is not a journey to remember with affection.

The summit from Grasmoor End

Skiddaw and Grisedale Pike from Grasmoor

VIA THE NORTH-WEST ARÊTE

The west and north sides of Grasmoor meet at a steep and rocky right-angled corner, clearly delineated on a sunny day by the edge of the dark shadow that shrouds the north side during most of the daylight hours, as is well shown on Derry's photograph on page 82. In mountaineering circles this corner would be called an arête.

I think I may claim to have pioneered this arête as a route to the summit, to which it obviously led directly. I had studied it from the road below for years before daring to venture upon it. When I finally did, with some trepidation, I found no cairns, no toffee papers, no orange peel, no evidence whatever that anyone had been there before. I felt I was treading virgin ground.

The details of the arête were difficult to assess from below. Above an initial scree slope, there appeared to be a succession of low crags all the way to the top. I started up in a state of excitement, fearing I would be faced by some insuperable obstacle that would turn me back. But all went well. Every rocky problem could be circumvented by a process of trial and error and only at one point where I had to squeeze through a crack in a low cliff, was success in doubt. I called this crack Fat Man's Agony since, at that time, I weighed sixteen stones and it was not easy to negotiate. Panic turned to pleasure as I slowly scrambled upwards, and it was with immense satisfaction that I ultimately set foot on the pinnacle of Grasmoor End and saw the summit within easy reach along a curving ridge.

The arête is by far the finest route of ascent but is for tough guys only. Sunday clothes, plastic shoes and a placid temperament would be certain casualties.

THE SUMMIT: 2791 FT

Many cairns adorn the ample top but the highest is not in doubt: it is a great heap of stones roughly shaped into compartments to serve as shelters from the wind. Nearby is a smaller windbreak of stones and, beyond, is the brink of the tremendous plunge of crags and scree on the west face, confirming the hopelessness of direct ascents on this side. It is a fearful sight better viewed from Grasmoor End which is reached by a short walk from the summit. There is a covering of small stones around the main cairn but this gives way to pleasant turf as the summit widens into a plateau eastwards.

The top is circumscribed by cliffs and routes of descent should be selected with care. The easiest lies along the descending east ridge to Coledale Hause. The Dove Crags and Lad Hows routes should not be attempted, especially in mist, and the north-west arête is out of the question in any weather condition. Red Gill, although accursed by overmuch scree, is a practicable and safe direct way down to the Buttermere valley.

Grasmoor's superior altitude gives it distinction as a viewpoint. The panorama from the summit cairn is uninterrupted and comprehensive, all the major heights in the district being revealed in a crowded horizon. The broad top, however, hides the surrounding valleys, the prospect being exclusively of distant mountain ranges. This deficiency, however, is remedied by a short walk to the edge of the west face where great depth is suddenly added to the scene, the prospect southwards being of classic quality and one of the finest in Lakeland.

Grasmoor's other shortcomings are forgiven when the summit is reached.

The view southwards from the top of Grasmoor's west face

Great Gable

2949 ft

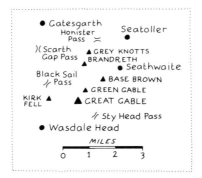

GREAT GABLE IS EVERYBODY'S favourite. The very name is a compelling magnet, the aspect of the mountain on all sides is challenging and its ascent a highlight in the itineraries of all active walkers in Lakeland. Great Gable caters for all sorts: youngsters find an exuberant delight in clambering to the top, novices serving their apprenticeship on the fells gain valuable experience, seasoned walkers often return to resume an intimate acquaintance, and intrepid rock-climbers aim for familiar crags in eager anticipation of exhilarating hours in their awesome and austere company.

The mountain is simple in structure, without complications, matching the popular concept of a mountain form: a steep-sided pyramid tapering to a slender top. Gable is all ups and downs, a huge cone of severe and uncompromising gradients with no halts in the steepness, no tracts of flat ground to relieve ascent or descent. Kirk Fell and Green Gable are close supporting neighbours, linked with the master at a high level but otherwise the mountain rises in supreme isolation, proud and independent, a massive cornerstone of the western fells.

It was the early dalesfolk of Wasdale Head who gave the mountain its apt name and they could not have chosen a more appropriate one for the imposing presence that closes and dominates their valley. Its finest aspect is from Wasdale Head, seen as a strong yet graceful tower with a summit defended by crags. From Lingmell Beck at its base, relentless slopes soar upwards for half a mile in a lateral distance of less than a mile, under a covering of stones and boulders and rock debris so extensive that the cliffs from which they fell in ages past must have been of far greater proportions than the remnants that remain today as the Great Napes. These slopes are an untrodden wasteland of scree at a high angle, an uninviting and arid desert. On the north side, too, the shadowed precipice of Gable Crag has shed fans of scree into the desolate gathering grounds of the River Liza. The east flank is more accommodating and it is on this side that walkers are offered a route of ascent that is the least arduous and has welcome vestiges of greenery amongst the stones. Direct approaches from the west are ruled out by further interminable slopes of scree.

Opposite *Great Gable from Wasdale*

Great Gable from Wasdale Head   Opposite *Great Gable from Kirk Fell*

Seldom does a day pass without visitors appearing on the summit yet, despite the popularity of the climb, walkers are severely constrained by the rugged texture of the ground, there being little incentive to stray from the few paths. Great Gable has not been tamed and never will be.

The boundaries of the mountain are well defined by the River Liza in the north, Gable Beck in the west and Lingmell Beck in the south, while its eastern roots are crossed by the Sty Head Pass. The steep slopes on all sides preclude the formation of tarns and, apart from a small pool, Dry Tarn, near the path from Sty Head but usually passed unnoticed, there are no gatherings of water within its limits. At Beck Head, where there is a link with Kirk Fell, there are small pools. In a hollow on the eastern base, below the impressive ravine of Aaron Slack, which also brings down a trickle of water, is the large expanse of Styhead Tarn.

The valleys of the Lake District have been robbed of their romantic charm by car and caravan parks, camp sites, time-share developments, leisure centres and commercial interests, and by the misguided efforts of the local Tourist Board to induce more visitors to come to the district. The valleys are losing their character and appeal through overkill. The mountain fastnesses must never be allowed to suffer by exploitation of their natural solitudes. Some years ago, there was an incredible plan put forward for a motor road to be made over Sty Head Pass; commonsense prevailed and the plans were overruled. If motorists want to pass from Borrowdale to Wasdale they must walk and the effort will do them more good. A motor road over Sty Head, doubtless with a large car park on the summit, would be the ultimate sacrilege and would be followed by a suggestion for a chair lift up Great Gable. Perish the thought – Great Gable has a dignity that must be respected. Fellwalkers are its trustees.

ASCENTS

There is little scope for exploration during the ascent of Great Gable and walkers are content to follow the few much-trodden paths to the summit without deviating into the rough terrain alongside. Nor is there much point in doing so.

VIA STY HEAD

The most frequented path, kicked to the width of a road by thousands of boots every year, leaves the top of Sty Head Pass and cannot be lost even in mist.

Sty Head is the best-known walkers' crossroads amongst the mountains with tracks radiating in all directions. It is reached from Wasdale Head by way of a stony path that slants upwards across the fellside, over-use having converted it into an ugly scar; or, more pleasantly, by the original Valley Route, which keeps alongside Lingmell Beck and finally scales grassy slopes to the top of the pass. From Seathwaite in Borrowdale the only instruction needed on a fine day is to follow the crowds above Stockley Bridge; or, more attractively, to take an alternative route alongside Taylorgill Force; this has found favour in recent years.

The path to the summit from Sty Head is unmistakable. This is known as the Breast Route and is so much in use that it might also be named the Tourist Route. It is a dull trudge to the top, without perils and without excitement, its single merit being that it scores a bull's-eye by arriving exactly at the summit cairn.

VIA AARON SLACK

On a day when the Breast Route is likely to be over-populated, a quiet alternative is offered by the tremendous ravine of Aaron Slack which emphatically divides Great Gable from Green Gable and is easily reached from the outflow of Styhead Tarn.

Aaron Slack is stony, dull, without views, deeply enclosed and claustrophobic but points the way directly to Windy Gap, the narrow col linking the two Gables. A path going off left from here, after a rocky scramble, reaches the summit plateau.

In the final stages, it is worth making a short detour to the edge of Gable Crag for the sensational views therefrom down into Stone Cove.

Sty Head from Lingmell

View from Green Gable

VIA SOURMILK GILL AND GREEN GABLE

An ascent is always more pleasurable if the climb is alongside the rapid fall of a mountain stream, and one of the most charming of such companions is Sourmilk Gill as it leaps and dances down a steep fellside to join the River Derwent at Seathwaite Bridge. A path goes up the south bank among a scattering of trees to reach the vast hollow of Gillercomb and curves around Base Brown, with Raven Crag, also called Gillercomb Buttress, an imposing sight across the stream. The path then gains a foothold on an easy ridge leading directly to the top of Green Gable. Great Gable is then only a stone's throw away, a massive object with the black cliffs of Gable Crag prominent. A five-minute descent leads to the near col of Windy Gap, which is crossed to a path skirting the cliffs and after a rocky passage leads on to the top of the mountain. Strictly this route is an ascent of Green Gable extended to Great Gable and may not satisfy the purist who prefers direct ascents without passing over intermediate summits; non-purists, however, will enjoy its solitude and interesting surroundings. It is greatly to be preferred to the Breast Route.

VIA HONISTER PASS

This is a route favoured by walkers who own cars; they can save themselves a thousand feet of climbing on foot by travelling to the top of Honister Pass on wheels and there find ample parking space. Initially the climb is steep and stony as it follows the line of an old tramway built originally to bring slates down from the quarry to the cutting sheds. At the head of the incline is the site of the drum house where the movement of the wagons was controlled, and at this point a broad path turns away south across open ground, gently rising below Grey Knotts and Brandreth and providing lovely views of the Buttermere valley before turning left to reach the summit of Green Gable along its north ridge. A short descent leads to Windy Gap and a final climb to the top of Great Gable. This route has the same defect as that via Sourmilk Gill, i.e. that it is not a direct ascent of Great Gable, but it is an exhilarating walk with splendid views.

Great Gable from Beck Head

VIA BECK HEAD FROM ENNERDALE

Because of its remoteness and isolation, the head of Ennerdale is not a usual starting point for the ascent of Great Gable although the mountain towers above the valley with such dominance and majesty that it transfixes attention.

From the Black Sail Youth Hostel, the River Liza is followed upstream to its confluence with the watercourse coming down from the depression of Beck Head; this is reached up a grassy and pathless slope. Here the north-west angle of the mountain is directly ahead and can be climbed by a steep and stony track to the top.

VIA GAVEL NEESE

Gavel Neese is the indefinite ridge formed by the south-west corner of the mountain, facing the approach from Wasdale Head. This offers the most direct way to the summit, but this is its only merit. Every step of the climb is relentlessly upwards, a strenuous and exhausting battle against gravity, of appeal only to the toughest of walkers.

The lower part of the Neese (nose) is grassy and pleasant but the slope becomes increasingly steep. When progress is barred by the rocks of White Napes, a move is made into the long scree gully of Little Hell Gate, a channel of stones adding further discomfort, and only when the top of the gully is gained at a short lateral ridge is anguish dissipated by smiles. The ridge leads to the final obstacle of Westmorland Crags, which is avoided by a scrambling path to the summit. Celebrations follow.

94

DESCENTS

All routes of ascent may be reversed but only with reservations. Paths must be adhered to closely; short cuts on Great Gable lead into trouble. The easiest way off, and the best in bad weather, is the Breast Route to Sty Head. Aaron Slack offers shelter from strong winds. Motorists who have to return to their cars on Honister Pass are recommended in clear weather to pass over the summits of Brandreth and Grey Knotts and descend directly from the latter. On other routes, walkers need to take especial care where the feet are placed; Great Gable suffers from a plague of stones and they do not take kindly to being trampled upon.

THE SUMMIT: 2949 FT

Rather unexpectedly, the summit is a broad, tilted plateau, and not at all the sharp peak suggested by its appearance from Wasdale. An untidy pile of rocks, surmounted by a cairn, marks the highest point. Affixed to a slab is the bronze War Memorial tablet of the Fell and Rock Climbing Club dedicated in 1924 and ever since the venue of an annual Remembrance Service held in November. It is usually attended by a congregation of hundreds of fellwalkers.

As I have recounted before, Great Gable's summit is rather special to me for a particular reason. In 1967, it came as a great surprise to me when I was awarded the MBE in recognition of the completion of my *Pictorial Guide to the Lakeland Fells*, which I had compiled between 1952 and 1966. It wasn't until 1980 that I learned from a correspondent that, fourteen years earlier, a fellwalker from Southport had spent the day on the summit of Great Gable collecting signatures to a petition which was later sent to Downing Street.

The Memorial Service on Great Gable: November 1989

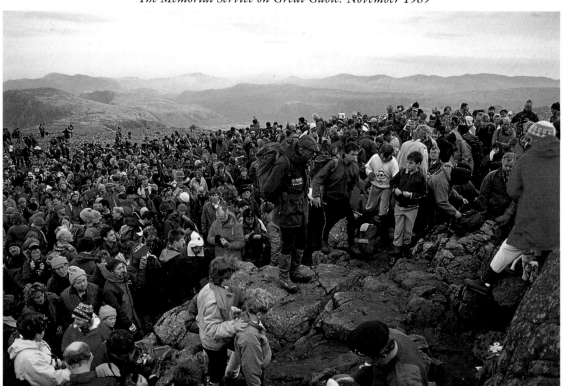

The summit of Great Gable Below *Westmorland Cairn*

An excellent panorama, rich in detail and extending to all points of the compass, rewards those who reach the summit. The view is predominantly of mountains and fells arranged in a distant circle, all the principal heights in the district being seen except the Coniston fells which are hidden by the Scafell range. Sprinkling Tarn and a few others are glimpsed, Wastwater is the only lake in sight. The radiating valleys of Eskdale, Wasdale, Ennerdale, Buttermere and Borrowdale carve their way through the high ground, adding a touch of greenery to a sombre picture.

A visit to the summit is incomplete without a short detour to Westmorland Cairn, a well-constructed pile of stones soon reached by walking in the direction of Wasdale. This was erected in 1876 by two brothers named Westmorland to mark what they considered to be the finest viewpoint in the district. Few will disagree. Wasdale Head is seen far below as from an aeroplane, a jigsaw pattern of walled fields around the inn and farmsteads and, beyond, the full length of Wastwater, the coast, the Irish Sea and the Isle of Man: a perfect composition. The Westmorland brothers were right.

MOSES' TROD

It is given to few men to be remembered in history by having their names preserved for posterity because of paths they originated and established, the only instance in Lakeland of such a distinction being earned by a colourful character known as Moses Rigg. Moses was employed at Honister Quarry in the days of primitive roads when the slates were transported by pony-drawn sleds. His regular tour of duty was to take such loads to Wasdale and the port of Ravenglass and he devised a high-level route across the mountains that led almost directly to Wasdale Head. He kept himself busy: after his day's work at the quarry, his practice was to illegally distil whisky using the bogwater nearby and he smuggled his potent produce with his loads of slate for sale on his journeys.

His route coincided initially with the present Great Gable path from the site of the Drum House, but beyond the Brandreth fence it continued straight ahead to ford the infant River Liza below Gable Crag, then slanted up to Beck Head and contoured the west slope of Great Gable to reach Gavel Neese. Here an upstanding rock still bears the name of Moses' Finger. Finally, there is an easy descent to Wasdale Head. His route was formerly known as Moses' Sledgate, but since its adoption in part by walkers, is commonly given the name of Moses' Trod. Also attributed to Moses was a stone hut on Gable Crag (the Smuggler's Retreat); when standing, this was the highest building in England but it is now crumbled to dust. A gully in the crag below was named Smuggler's Chimney after its first ascent in 1909 in deference to Moses' memory.

Buttermere from Moses' Trod

Tophet Bastion   Below *Kern Knotts*

THE GABLE GIRDLE

Great Gable lends itself admirably to a circular walk at mid-height around its flanks, starting and finishing at Sty Head; the walk provides an exciting journey during the course of which all the crags and rock formations that so distinguish the mountain are visited at close range, even intimately, yet in safety. Furthermore, the walk maintains a fairly level contour and there is no steep climbing. The ground underfoot is rough, however, and the expedition is not to be undertaken lightly. On a day when a proposed ascent to the summit is aborted by low cloud on the top, this circular tour is an excellent alternative, revealing graphic scenes of rock architecture that escape notice on visits to the top. No other mountain is so accommodating in sharing its secrets.

I call this walk the Gable Girdle.

The circuit starts at Sty Head and the easiest progress is made by following the route in a clockwise direction. A track leaves the top of the pass a few paces to the left of the start of the Breast Route. This track was originally used exclusively by rockclimbers as a route of access to the Great Napes and for many years the initial twenty yards were deliberately left untrodden to avoid confusion with the walkers' path up the Breast.

The Girdle Path to Kern Knotts   Below *Wasdale from Great Hell Gate*

The track descends slightly and almost immediately the great buttress of Kern Knotts appears across the line of march, seemingly impassable. The vertical face of this formidable wall of rock is split from top to bottom by the famous Kern Knotts Crack, a severe test for cragsmen but happily not part of the Girdle itinerary. The base of the buttress is a wild tumble of large boulders, negotiable with extreme care, some gymnastic skill being needed to reach easier ground beyond. Here a track again forms below impending cliffs and then rises gradually across the fellside.

With the serrated turrets of the Great Napes now beckoning ahead, the track picks a stony way towards them, passing a small cave where a trickle of water, a rarity on Gable, provides the only liquid sustenance until Aaron Slack is reached.

Excitement increases when a wide scree gully appears across the route. This is Great Hell Gate, a river of stones in the middle of which will be seen, looking up, the solitary rock fang of Hell Gate Pillar.

Bounding the gully on the far side is the tremendous rock wall of Tophet Bastion, a forerunner of the Great Napes.

The Cat Rock and the Napes ridge   Below *Napes Needle*

Across Great Hell Gate, the track rises and then levels along the base of the soaring towers and ridges of the Great Napes and here walkers are privileged to see at close quarters one of the most popular rockclimbing grounds in the district with a near-vertical network of routes of ascent far beyond the capacity of non-professional climbers who can only stand aghast at the daring and courage of those proficient in the sport and feel, as I do, an inferior species.

Here too is a slender detached pinnacle of rock of international renown, the famous Napes Needle. It stands at the base of the crags and is not readily identifiable from the track below: walkers intent on watching where they are putting their feet are likely to pass it unnoticed. A scramble of twenty yards up the slope alongside reveals its proportions and supreme isolation perfectly, and from a terrace on the rocks opposite, known as the Dress Circle and used as a gallery by onlookers witnessing its ascent, it makes an irresistible subject for the camera.

The cliffs end abruptly beyond a prominent upstanding rock on the skyline known variously as the Cat or Sphinx Rock, and another river of scree is encountered. This is Little Hell Gate.

At Little Hell Gate there is an opportunity for a change of purpose, the summit being accessible from this point by turning up the stony channel of the Gate. To continue the Girdle, however, the scree is crossed laterally, the track becoming less distinct as it rounds the base of the White Napes where the rocks are more broken and less well defined, and curves north across the west flank, maintaining an even contour. Here is a new landscape, Kirk Fell, rising steeply above the descending stream of Gable Beck. The next objective is the ridge formed by the north-western corner of the mountain above the depression of Beck Head. This ridge carries a rough path to the summit but is crossed where two cairns indicate the continuance of the Girdle track, which passes between them and rises towards the dark and forbidding cliffs of Gable Crag. Here it skirts their lower rocks and provides awesome glimpses of the gullies splitting the face of the huge precipice above. From this elevated traverse, there is a splendid view of Green Gable across the bouldery hollow of Stone Cove, its neat top supported by a long line of cliffs. The track descends slightly as the crags decline and a short scramble brings Windy Gap underfoot.

Windy Gap is crossed by the familiar path from Honister and over its narrow crest commences the final descent, easy slopes leading down into the great rift of Aaron Slack, becoming deeply enclosed. The bed of this ravine is choked by stones and progress is slow but cheered by the appearance of a stream. Clear of the ravine, easy grass goes down to the outlet of Styhead Tarn.

This completes the circuit of a fine mountain, an interesting and thrilling walk that earns for Great Gable a fuller appreciation and respect.

Gable Crag from Green Gable

Haystacks

1900 ft

SOME MISINFORMED SOURCES HAVE defined a mountain as a hill which exceeds 2000 feet in height. Of course they are wrong. The status of mountain is not determined by any arbitrary level of altitude but by appearance. Rocks and ruggedness, roughness of terrain and a commanding presence are the essential qualifications. I prefer the definition in my old dictionary: 'a large mass of earth and rock rising above the adjacent land'. Those who say that Haystacks is not a mountain because it does not top 2000 feet should go and see it. Or better still, climb it; Haystacks would be mortally offended if classed merely as a hill. Everything expected of a mountain is here in full measure: rocks, crags, bogs, runnels of water, tarns, boulders, scree and glorious views.

Haystacks stands in the company of Great Gable and Pillar and although a thousand feet lower does not admit to any sense of inferiority; as is often the case with the smallest terrier in a pack, it is pugnacious, aggressive, demands attention and is subservient to nothing and nobody.

Early guidebook writers gave scant recognition to Haystacks, mentioning it only briefly and without recommendation and not until after the last war, with the rapid development of fellwalking, was a clear path trodden to the summit and along the length of the top. No longer neglected, Haystacks has now become a first objective. The Cinderella of Buttermere has blossomed into a prima donna. Today, Haystacks has a growing army of devotees. The savage little beast has been discovered to have lovable qualities.

The curious name is derived from the columnar buttresses that range in a series of rock towers along the northern fringe of the summit, the largest of these being known as Big Stack. The west side is steep and stony but is soon halted by Scarth Gap. There is a free fall in the south to the head of Ennerdale, this flank too being rough and uninviting. Only to the east is there easy ground, an indefinite ridge rising gradually to Brandreth, marked by the stanchions of a vanished wire fence.

It is the area between its boundaries that fascinates. Below the summit and away from the path is a wild and undisciplined tangle of heather, rocky tors and outcrops, perched boulders, crags, marshes and pools with no semblance of tidy arrangement but a delight to explore. Minor undulations abound and every corner reveals a fresh surprise. And, best of all, the colourful top is bejewelled by two lovely tarns, Innominate Tarn and Blackbeck Tarn; all around are entrancing views.

If mountains had fan clubs, Haystacks would have a legion of members. And I would be the first to enrol.

Opposite *Haystacks from Warnscale Bottom*

Haystacks from Scarth Gap Pass

ASCENTS

There are two usual routes of ascent, each served by paths that grow wider every year, and a third, unfrequented and more adventurous but best of all.

FROM GATESGARTH VIA SCARTH GAP

The path from Gatesgarth joins another coming along the south-west shore of Buttermere near the head of the lake and the grassy slopes of High Crag are then ascended to Scarth Gap. From a point near the path before reaching the Gap, there is a near view of Big Stack, the forerunner of the northern cliffs and a good advocate of their immensity. At Scarth Gap a steep and much corroded path turns left to the summit, passing a charming rocky pool on the way. This final path has suffered severely from the tread of boots, so much so that wardens have fashioned rough steps to contain the traffic. This I deplore. Steps are for going upstairs, not for climbing mountains. Erosion of paths is a growing problem and the remedy is to educate people to walk circumspectly and in single file, keeping strictly to the path and not trampling the verges. It is wrong to castigate the guidebook writers.

FROM HONISTER

A longer route, traversing the top from end to end and giving a better appraisal of the mountain, starts from the top of Honister Pass and climbs the old tramway and goes forward to the disused Dubs Quarry, where a track turns off to cross the shallow depression of Dubs Bottom, fording Warnscale Beck and rises to the crest of Green Crag. From this vantage point Haystacks is seen ahead in all its glory. The track descends to ford the outflow of Blackbeck Tarn and rises amidst impressive surroundings to Innominate Tarn, skirting its shore on a final climb to the summit cairn.

This route lends itself to a thrilling deviation. Before reaching Innominate Tarn, the rough ground on the right is crossed to the brink of the northern cliffs, with sensational views down to Warnscale Bottom and the Buttermere valley, and by following the precipitous edge westwards the cairn is reached in a state of excitement just above Big Stack. These cliffs or stacks are the greatest feature on the mountain but remain unseen by those who keep strictly to the path.

From the cairn the full traverse is completed by a descent to Scarth Gap.

FROM GATESGARTH VIA WARNSCALE BOTTOM

The Ordnance Survey maps issued in 1901 on the generous scale of six inches to a mile provide a wealth of detail since sacrificed on the later small-scale maps; in particular, they showed the roads made to service the quarries and mines on the fells, most of which had ceased operation before the turn of the century. Many of these old roads and track ways can still be seen and followed although they too have fallen into disuse through neglect. Invariably they were well graded to ease the passage of horses and carts and, where they can be found, often ease the passage of modern walkers too.

It was such a reference on the 1901 map that sent me in search of the old quarry road coming down into Warnscale Bottom from a quarry high on Green Crag. All walkers know the distinct quarry road from Dubs through Warnscale Bottom but the map indicated another on the other side of the descending beck, not seen from a distance and probably totally forgotten. Easy to trace when found, this route provides the finest and most interesting approach to Haystacks.

Warnscale Bottom is entered above the intake wall from Gatesgarth, the Dubs track being left and Warnscale Beck forded just above its confluence with Black Beck which pours down a huge cleft in the crags high on the right. Here the old road or cart-track to Green Crag Quarry will be found and can be followed uphill in a most delightful series of zigzags, still distinct after two centuries of non-use. Beyond the quarry, a short pathless scramble joins the path coming from Dubs Quarry for the final mile to the top.

This route, more than any other, gives a full appreciation of Haystacks.

Haystacks from Green Crag

Innominate Tarn

The Summit: 1900 ft

The Ordnance surveyors, like the guidebook writers, seem to have regarded Haystacks as insignificant in earlier times and did not trouble to give it a spot height, 1900 feet being my own estimate.

The highest point occurs at the western end. There is nothing neat and formal about Haystacks and the cairn has the same characteristics, being an untidy heap of stones loosely thrown together on a rocky plinth.

Descents from the mountain should be made only along the recognised paths to Scarth Gap or Dubs Quarry; exploratory descents are likely to lead to desperate situations.

Because of its low elevation, views from Haystacks are restricted by the ring of higher peaks all around and only to the north and east are distant horizons glimpsed, formed by Skiddaw and the Helvellyn range; otherwise the prospect from the summit is severely circumscribed. Nearby, and seen in intimate detail, are Great Gable, Pillar, High Crag, Grasmoor, Robinson and Dale Head, all looking down patronisingly at the shaggy little mountain in their midst.

The gem of the view is the Buttermere valley and its lakes, better seen from the edge of the northern cliffs or from the top of the great cleft containing the outflow of Blackbeck Tarn.

Above *The summit cairn*   Below *The Buttermere Valley*

Helvellyn

3148 ft

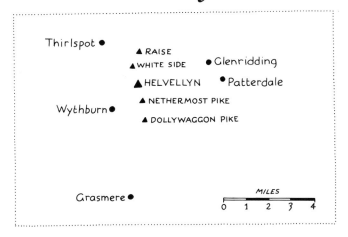

IF STATISTICS WERE AVAILABLE, they would probably confirm that Helvellyn is the Lakeland mountain most often climbed and the best known by name to the visiting public; the ascent is frequently made by people who perhaps climb Helvellyn and no other mountain. This fame has not been achieved by any outstanding qualities nor grace of outline nor a challenging appeal: in fact, the mountain appears from most directions as a shapeless mass of high ground lacking a distinctive summit and is buttressed by equally unattractive neighbours. Yet there are good reasons for the popularity of Helvellyn: it is one of the small and select company exceeding 3000 feet in altitude; it is very conveniently situated alongside the busy main road through the district; legend and poetry have invested the lovely name with an air of romance; and in Striding Edge it has a spectacular highlight that is a prime objective for fellwalkers. Furthermore, the summit has a long-established reputation as the best viewpoint for witnessing the sunrise, and ascents in late evening and in darkness are unique to Helvellyn.

The top is the highest part of a long mountain range extending from Grisedale Tarn in the south to Threlkeld Common in the north, the whole forming an immense natural barrier of high ground for several miles with no road crossing and only one continuous path, over Sticks Pass, by which pedestrians can pass from one side to the other. The full traverse of the range therefore presents a greater challenge than does the ascent of Helvellyn alone, no fewer than ten distinct summits being visited along the way.

The western boundary of the range is formed by Thirlmere and St John's in the Vale, and the eastern by Ullswater. In views of the mountain from the valleys, the two lakes do their best to add a little charm to the harsh slopes rising above but fail to do so. Helvellyn goes in for strength, not beauty.

Opposite *Helvellyn from St Sunday Crag*

The western aspect of Helvellyn and its close supporters is dull and disappointing; steep convex slopes rise out of the Thirlmere plantations and have the appearance from afar of a herd of sleeping elephants – there is little to excite interest and nothing at all to suggest that other aspects are not similarly placid and uneventful.

But the eastern side of this mountain group is very different. Here the long summit ridge is seen to collapse in a series of shattered cliffs from which fans of scree pour into deep hollows, a stark manifestation of the natural forces that ended the Ice Age. Then composure is restored and the ground declines more gently to the shores of Ullswater. In this wild upper scene, where the desolation is profound, two bony arms protrude from Helvellyn's summit to clasp between them the silent waters of Red Tarn, deeply inurned amongst a grim surround of rocks and scree. These two arms are Striding Edge and Swirral Edge, the first-named a narrow crest of naked rock poised high above fearful declivities and of national renown and the second a less definite descending ridge.

South of the summit, the fall of land is soon interrupted by a short rise to the flat top of Nethermost Pike, this also having innocuous slopes to the west and precipitous cliffs to the east. Below the latter, in the stony depths of Ruthwaite Cove, is the delightful pool of Hard Tarn, rarely noticed and rarely visited, quite remote from beaten tracks.

Helvellyn across Thirlmere

Walkers on Striding Edge, from Red Tarn

North of the summit is the subsidiary top of Helvellyn Lower Man, beyond which the ground drops sharply to the next height in the range, White Side, which also has grassy western slopes but is scarped on the east flank above the now dry bed of Keppel Cove Tarn. This was formerly used as a reservoir for the large Greenside Mine but was drained and abandoned when the works closed; the breached dam is one of the few industrial relics remaining in the Helvellyn group.

Streams flowing west from the range enter Thirlmere or St John's Beck on their way to join the River Greta: those flowing east enter Ullswater and the River Eamont. There is a notable waterfall in Fisher Gill, seen on the old pony route from Thirlspot: the other principal watercourses are Raise Beck, Whelpside Gill and Helvellyn Gill in the west, and Red Tarn Beck in the east.

Helvellyn was a favourite objective of visitors to the district in Victorian times and its ascent considered to be a commendable achievement calling for celebrations. It was the common practice in those early days to make the climb on the backs of ponies wth a local guide in attendance, and paths were made for safe passage. But by the turn of the century, the apprehension and fear once inspired by Helvellyn had faded as more adventurous walkers made their way to the top on foot and returned without mishaps, their numbers increasing year after year. Today Helvellyn is regarded as a benign friend by the thousands of happy wanderers who perambulate the paths and summit as pilgrims to a shrine.

View from Helvellyn's summit to Nethermost and Dollywaggon Pikes

ASCENTS

The Victorians had a choice between two pony routes to take them to the top of Helvellyn. Today's visitors can select from seven continuous paths, all indicated on the Ordnance Survey maps, and a few other ways not so recognised. It is unfortunate that most of these routes start from the A591 road along the western base, ascents on this side being dull and tedious and not to be compared in interest and scenic values with the climbs from the east.

FROM GRASMERE VIA GRISEDALE HAUSE

This ascent is an adaptation for walkers of the former pony route and takes advantage of the prepared and graded path in popular use last century. It leaves the main road at Mill Bridge and climbs to Grisedale Hause with no sighting thus far of the objective. At the Hause, however, the Helvellyn massif is suddenly revealed, with Dollywaggon Pike in full view across the waters of Grisedale Tarn. From the outlet of the tarn the pony route, now blazed white by boots, ascends the Pike in a series of zigzags but bypasses the summit to continue forward to Nethermost Pike and thence to the summit. There are impressive downward views of Nethermost Cove and Striding Edge on the final rise to the top. Not until the easy section of the ridge beyond Dollywaggon Pike is reached does the walker feel justly rewarded for his efforts on a tedious climb, the dramatic views eastwards being a full recompense.

FROM DUNMAIL RISE VIA GRISEDALE TARN

A shorter way to Grisedale Tarn is available from Dunmail Raise on the A591 with the added advantage of a higher start. This route goes up alongside Raise Beck, which originally descended to Grasmere exclusively but has been diverted in part to flow north to feed Thirlmere since its conversion to a reservoir. Raise Beck is a jolly companion in a rocky channel as it leads to marshy ground at Grisedale Tarn. Here the pony route from Grasmere can be joined at the foot of Dollywaggon Pike.

Helvellyn Gill and Browncove Crags

FROM WYTHBURN

This popular route has been provided at its starting point with a car park near Wythburn Church on the edge of Thirlmere and there are few days in the year when it is not well patronised, this is also the way most usually followed by those wanting to watch the sun rise. Apart from its convenience and directness, there is little to commend it, the climb being initially very steep although eased by zigzags, and there is no relief until the higher ground is reached and the gradients become more amenable. The pony route from Grasmere is joined in the depression on the ridge between Helvellyn and Nethermost Pike for the final simple walk to the top. The only highlight on this rather uninteresting climb occurs at the point where the Grasmere route is joined and sensational views eastwards are revealed.

FROM THE A591 VIA THE OLD LEAD MINES

This is the most direct route of all and the most arduous on rough terrain without the help of a path. The lone walker who prefers his own company to that of the perspiring crowds on the Wythburn path will find this route ideal: it carries a guarantee that no other bodies will be met or even seen until the summit is reached. The A591 is left half a mile north of Wythburn, an open field between plantations being crossed to a nameless stream, which is then followed very steeply upwards, passing the ruins of old lead mines, to its source on easier ground below the summit. By veering right in the final stages, Brownrigg Well, the spring that supplies Whelpside Gill, may be found.

FROM THE A591 VIA HELVELLYN GILL

When I first came this way there was no vestige of a path but in recent times one has blossomed to such an extent that it is clearly visible from the road, its increasing use no doubt having been occasioned by the making of a roadside car park near the starting point. Across the road, the plantations are skirted to come alongside Helvellyn Gill, where a track is then climbed to meet the White Stones path (described next) on the steep rise to Browncove Crags, the walk to the summit then being a simple march.

FROM THIRLSPOT VIA THE WHITE STONES PATH

For many years after this route had become well established, confusion was caused to walkers by the Ordnance Survey's omission to acknowledge its existence on their maps, which continued to show the old pony route as the only way from Thirlspot long after it had fallen into neglect and disuse.

The White Stones route starts above the intake wall behind the King's Head at Thirlspot, the path being indicated by a succession of wayside stones, whitewashed periodically, up the initial steep slope. The path then turns along an easy shelf before it rises and is joined by the Helvellyn Gill route for the climb up the side of Browncove Crags and so to the summit.

On recent maps, the Ordnance Survey show the path as passing below Browncove Crags and not over them as previously. This may be a mistake on their part, which is almost unthinkable although they have been known to err on infrequent occasions, or it may be to discourage walkers from climbing the unstable scree on the former route where there is severe erosion.

FROM THIRLSPOT VIA THE OLD PONY ROUTE

Paths made for the passage of ponies carrying humans had necessarily to be gently graded and avoid steep pitches, and to meet these requirements the route from Thirlspot followed a roundabout course, making a wide loop above the intake wall behind the King's Head to come alongside Fisher Gill. It then crosses the easy western slopes of White Side and mounts the ridge to Helvellyn Lower Man, a few minutes from the summit.

This route can still be traced although it is now indistinct in places and intermittent: it has the merit of quiet seclusion.

Ullswater and the Pennines seen from Helvellyn

FROM GLENRIDDING VIA RED TARN

The motor road to the abandoned Greenside Lead Mine, which has disappeared under a carpet of grass, is succeeded by a path following the course of Glenridding Beck upstream towards the huge cone of Catstycam. This is forded when Red Tarn Beck joins in from the left and proves an infallible guide to the large expanse of Red Tarn in a deep hollow below Helvellyn. The path then rises to Swirral Edge, forming a ladder of stones to the summit.

   Catstycam dominates this route and its neat summit is really too good to miss. It can be reached by a direct climb from Glenridding Beck by walkers of abundant energy, this being the longest, the roughest and the steepest climb in the area with no hint of a path and no evidence that anyone has done it before. Or it can be reached, much more easily, by turning up the ridge from Swirral Edge to its summit.

FROM PATTERDALE VIA STRIDING EDGE

This is the finest way of all to the top of Helvellyn, a classic ascent recorded and underlined in the diaries of all fellwalkers in Lakeland and giving newcomers and novices a thrilling first taste of real mountaineering.

Looking down on Striding Edge

The Dixon Memorial

The Grisedale no-through road turns off the A592 near Patterdale church and rises gently to the terminus of tarmac, a fact invariably emphasised by an assortment of parked cars. From this point, Grisedale Beck is crossed to a path slanting upwards across the steep fellside of Birkhouse Moor leading to a ridge where easy progress is dramatically halted by the rocky turret of High Spying How, heralding the start of Striding Edge. Now, in a state of great exhilaration and excitement, with the adrenalin running high and a keen awareness of imminent danger, the rocky spine of the Edge is traversed to its end. At first it passes over flat slabs and then by a path a few feet below the crest; a stony climb beyond leads to the top of the mountain with the highest point nearby.

STRIDING EDGE

Striding Edge deserves more than a passing mention. Here in ages past natural forces of ice and storm have sculptured a narrow spine of rock some 300 yards in length, elevated high above awesome declivities of crag and scree yet leaving a safe passage along its crest.

Early writers regarded the Edge as a place of terror, and as recently as the mid-nineteenth century visitors were warned that its crossing was 'a foolhardy thing to do' and to be attempted only by 'steady mountaineers'.

But attitudes change with the times. Today Striding Edge is considered great fun and is 'conquered' by walkers of all ages, often in procession. In fact, queues often form at either end. Nevertheless, although quite safe in calm weather and even in mist, the Edge should be avoided in gales or when under snow and ice. In such conditions it is not fun, and Red Tarn and Swirral Edge provide a safer alternative.

THE HELVELLYN MONUMENTS

No mountain is more prolific than Helvellyn in visual reminders of past events connected with it, these being a measure of the reverence and respect in which it has been held over many years.

THE ROCK OF NAMES

When Thirlmere was a natural lake, before its conversion to a reservoir, the road along its eastern shore ran close by the water's edge and near it was a rock on which Wordsworth and Southey and Coleridge had carved their initials. The reservoir submerged the old road and the inscribed rock, which had become known as the Rock of Names was moved to a high bank alongside the new road at a higher level; tragically it was broken in transit and the fragments were piled into a cairn which remains to this day but is difficult to identify.

THE DIXON MEMORIAL

This commemorates the fatal fall from Striding Edge of a dalesman named Dixon while foxhunting, and is situated on a rock platform on the Edge overlooking Nethermost Cove: it is often passed unnoticed by walkers intent on watching precisely where they are placing their feet on the rough path. The memorial was erected in 1858.

THE GOUGH MEMORIAL

The best-known monument stands at the top of the rise from Striding Edge and is dedicated to Charles Gough who was killed in a fall while climbing Helvellyn from Patterdale on a spring day in 1805, accompanied by his dog. His body was not found until three months later, by a shepherd. The dog was still guarding his master's corpse as it doubtless had done ever since his death. The discovery aroused wide interest and prompted both Wordsworth and Scott to write poems paying touching tributes to the dog's fidelity. The monument was erected in 1890.

THE HINCKLER MEMORIAL

In 1926 Bert Hinckler landed an aeroplane on the top of Helvellyn, a feat considered to be so remarkable at the time that a stone tablet commemorating the event was erected by the side of the Wythburn path near the summit. It stands in a rash of stones and is sometimes obscured by them.

THE BROTHERS' PARTING

On the bouldery slope just below the outlet of Grisedale Tarn is an inscribed rock marking the place where, in 1805, Wordsworth parted from his sailor brother John, who was later lost at sea.

THE SUMMIT: 3148 FT

There can never be any doubt when the summit of Helvellyn is reached, even in the thickest mist, identification being confirmed by a large wind-shelter of stone walls built originally for the comfort of the Victorian pony trekkers.

The highest point is a small rise alongside occupied not by a handsome cairn as might be expected on so proud a mountain but by an insignificant and untidy heap of stones, a defect due to the absence of suitable building material on a top covered only by fragments of shale. There is also an absence of natural perches on which to sit and visitors invariably drift to the wind-shelter, which unfortunately accumulates the debris of countless packed lunches. An Ordnance column is nearby.

Liquid refreshment is available at Brownrigg Well, the highest spring in Lakeland and the source of Whelpside Gill which is situated a quarter of a mile due west of the summit down an easy slope.

The broad top is a simple promenade, well blazed by the paths to Wythburn and Thirlspot, both offering foolproof routes of descent.

Anyone who achieves the summit will be disappointed if the view is obscured by haze but will be delighted in conditions of clear visibility, since the prospect ranges over the whole of Lakeland with all the major peaks splendidly arrayed for inspection. Sunrise visitors must take a chance: night of stars is often succeeded by banks of mist at dawn.

The view is almost exclusively of mountains, the western horizons in particular being tightly crowded with them, but Ullswater is seen as a silver streak and there is even a glimpse of Morecambe Bay. Most interest will, however, be centred on the more intimate outlook over the eastern flank of the mountain, a dramatic revelation of the coves and ridges abutting against the summit but far below: a harsh landscape better viewed from the edge of the cliffs plunging down to Red Tarn. The Lower Man too commands new vistas and is easily reached. 'A savage place', said Wordsworth of this side of Helvellyn and those who look down on it from the top will certainly agree.

Above *The summit of Helvellyn*   Below *Striding Edge*

THE HELVELLYN RANGE

Scott wrote of 'the mighty Helvellyn' and if the mountain's domain is deemed to extend from Grisedale Tarn to Sticks Pass, where for several miles a high altitude is maintained, it is the mightiest of all, more massive even than Scafell Pike. But the area as so defined includes many subsidiary heights which, although closely allied to Helvellyn and forming part of the whole, have individual summits, some of them often visited on the ascent of Helvellyn and others retaining a degree of independence and deserving of separate expeditions.

DOLLYWAGGON PIKE: 2810 FT

Dollywaggon Pike is invariably climbed on the way to Helvellyn by the pony route from Grisedale Tarn, a dull trudge. A much grander and more interesting route is available, although pathless, by climbing the rough fellside from Ruthwaite Lodge on Grisedale Pass and joining a clearly defined ridge, The Tongue, that ascends unerringly to the neat summit between the stony hollows of Cock Cove and Ruthwaite Cove. Old mine levels will be seen in the stream bed near the lodge and as height is gained the tremendous shadowed cliffs of Dollywaggon Pike, Falcon Crag and Tarn Crag, not seen from the pony route, are fully revealed, an impressive sight. This is by far the best approach to the Pike and has the further merit of being lonely and unfrequented.

NETHERMOST PIKE: 2920 FT

This too is part of the tourist route to Helvellyn, but may also be climbed by a more exciting route rising out of Nethermost Cove, following the descending beck upwards until the east ridge of the Pike comes into view and then moving across to it. Nearby in Ruthwaite Cove is the rock-girt Hard Tarn in perfect solitude: here I once spent a lazy sunny day watching newts playing and hunting for flies in the crystal waters. The ridge looks daunting, a tower of rock, but there is no difficulty in climbing and scrambling up its spine to the flat summit.

CATSTYCAM: 2917 FT

Continuing the traverse northwards, Helvellyn's top is crossed to the point where Swirral Edge descends sharply towards Red Tarn. Swirral Edge is a poor second to Striding Edge but can be dangerous in icy conditions; Swirral Edge points the way to an easy ridge leading up to the neat summit of Catstycam, formerly known as Catchedicam which, although off the main ridge, offers quiet repose and, incidentally, has the only graceful peak in the group and the best view of Red Tarn and the two Edges.

HELVELLYN LOWER MAN: 3033 FT

Across a shallow depression on the top of Helvellyn and at the edge of the summit plateau is the Lower Man, commanding a view of the range which continues north. It is a prominent object when approached from that direction, indeed appearing to be the true summit. It is visited on the ascent from Thirlspot via the old pony route and is unavoidable on ascents from other points on the range to the north. It is unthinkable, however, that the Lower Man would ever be the sole objective of an expedition with the true summit clearly in view and only five minutes' easy walking distant. From the Lower Man, there is a pronounced fall as the main ridge descends to a depression and then rises to the next height in the range, White Side.

WHITE SIDE: 2832 FT

White Side is not particularly distinguished, its sprawling western side being featureless except for a proliferation of stones bearing veins of white quartz from which the name of the fell was derived. The eastern side is steeper and looks down on the breached dam and dry bed of Keppel Cove Tarn. Unexpectedly there is a clear zigzag path to the summit from Glenridding Beck.

RAISE: 2889 FT

The next height north of White Side is Raise, a fell with rather more character. The western slopes are a popular winter skiing ground; midway down its eastern side there was, until recently, an industrial chimney stack marking the end of an underground flue from the Glenridding Lead Mine, which is now closed. I remember Raise as the fell that gave me most trouble when I was trying to record the panorama from the summit, eight visits being necessary before I had a day of clear all-round visibility.

Beyond Raise the range is crossed by Sticks Pass and although the range continues for some miles, surveillance is taken over from Helvellyn by Great Dodd, 2807 ft.

BIRKHOUSE MOOR: 2350 FT

Standing apart from the main ridge but under the dominance of Helvellyn, Birkhouse Moor extends eastwards from Red Tarn as a shoulder of the mountain. Steep slopes decline to Ullswater, interrupted only by the little promontory of Keldas, very popular with visitors to Glenridding, the principal attractions here being the lovely tree-fringed Lanty's Tarn and a glorious view of Ullswater. Keldas is a little bit of heaven dropped on earth.

Ullswater from Keldas

High Stile

2644 ft

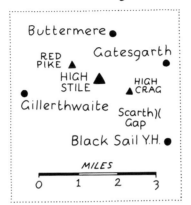

HIGH STILE IS THE pivot, the central point and the loftiest of a closely knit trinity of peaks on an elevated ridge between Buttermere and Ennerdale. But the ridge cannot be dismissed as merely a mountain barrier separating the two valleys. When walked from end to end, scenes of absorbing interest are revealed, contributed by the succession of vast hollows gouged out of the fellside immediately below a narrow crest, by the three distinctive summits and not least by the exquisite views on display all the way along. No artist, however great his talent, could possibly picture on canvas the glory of the Buttermere valley as seen aerially from the ridge. The rewards of a visit to High Stile more than compensate for the effort of getting there.

The Ennerdale side of the ridge, rising steeply out of the conifer plantations, holds litle promise of the excitement to come when the ridge is attained and is rarely climbed, all the scenic values being centred on the sculpturing of the Buttermere flank. High Stile presents a savage front on this side, a wild confusion of crags soaring above scree slopes from the lakeside trees and offering no invitation at all for a direct ascent. Its rocky summit is invariably reached after first ascending one of the others in the trinity, High Crag or Red Pike, and because all three are linked by easy walking, the usual practice is to include them all in a single expedition.

The graceful dome of Red Pike is a popular objective for walkers from Buttermere, the path there passing Bleaberry Tarn and then slanting upwards and becoming so eroded by the trampling of boots that it can be seen from afar as a white gash along the fellside. High Crag is a different proposition, a precipitous fall of crags from its summit giving the appearance of inaccessibility.

The dry and arid Ennerdale slopes do not carry watercourses; all the streams descend northwards to augment the lovely lakes of Buttermere and Crummock Water, the best known being the picturesque Sourmilk Gill, falling a thousand feet as a silver streak. Bleaberry Tarn, its source, is the only tarn, but in Scale Force the ridge can boast the highest waterfall in the district.

*Opposite **High Stile from Buttermere***

Bleaberry Comb

The features that add special distinction to the High Stile ridge are the immense hollows scooped out of it on the Buttermere side. These deep recesses are known locally as combs and elsewhere in the district as coves. The two most familiar to walkers are Bleaberry Comb between High Stile and Red Pike and containing Bleaberry Tarn, and Burtness (or Birkness) Comb between High Stile and High Crag, with no pedestrian paths but highly favoured by rock-climbers whose activities are catered for by Eagle Crag and Grey Crag. A third, Ling Comb, north of Red Pike, is less impressive and rarely visited.

ASCENTS

Direct beeline ascents of High Stile from Buttermere are ruled out by the hostile terrain, and from Ennerdale by the dense plantations of conifer and a forest fence.

There are, however, two feasible routes from Buttermere by which the summit may be reached without first passing over Red Pike or High Crag: these are pathless and for adventurous spirits only. One uses the climbers' track into Burtness Comb and departs from it to ascend the slope on the right, to reach a shoulder of High Stile that can be followed upwards over Grey Crag to the summit. The other crosses the marshy wastes beyond Bleaberry Tarn and climbs a scree gully of Chapel Crags to gain the ridge near the summit, or alternatively passes below Chapel Crags to easier ground on the north-east slope above all difficulties.

But almost invariably the summit is reached along the ridge, usually from Red Pike.

VIA RED PIKE

From Buttermere a path leaves the bridge near the outflow of the lake and makes a wide loop to the left to ease the steepness before reversing on a higher shelf to Bleaberry Tarn, where the slanting path to the top of Red Pike, which I remember as a thin track, is now so wide and obvious that only a genius could miss it.

Also a pathless way to the top, with the merit of undisturbed solitude a consideration on busy summer days, is by climbing alongside Far Ruddy Beck from Crummock Water into Ling Comb, there bearing left to the saddle below the top.

Or, more in favour, Red Pike can be climbed after the customary pilgrimage to Scale Force by a thin track rising to Lingcomb edge and the summit.

Or, from Ennerdale, by a path passing through a breach in the plantations near High Gillerthwaite, this leading directly but uneventfully to the highest cairn.

To reach the summit of High Stile, follow the route given on page 129, but in reverse direction.

Red Pike from High Stile

Buttermere from High Crag

VIA HIGH CRAG

High Crag is well named, a huge wall of rock falling from the summit through a vertical height of 500 feet towards Buttermere and making a direct assault totally out of the question. The usual route to the top leaves the Scarth Gap path when the crags are passed and tackles the steep scree slope of Gamlin End; this leads straight to the summit but only after a laborious and unpleasant ascent over loose and sliding stones. This was not to my liking at all and I began to cast around for a better alternative.

Then one day when walking in Burtness Comb I noticed a fault in the wall of rock that appeared to slant upwards from bottom to top with no obvious break. Upon investigation, I found myself on a rising grass shelf, narrow and littered by fallen boulders that led without difficulties to the north top of the mountain with the summit only minutes away. I called this route Sheepbone Rake after a nearby crag known as Sheepbone Buttress. The Rake is pathless with a sense of danger that does not happen and is infinitely to be preferred to Gamlin End.

To reach the summit of High Stile, follow the route given on page 129.

Sheepbone Crags

Buttermere from Burtness Comb

THE SUMMIT: 2644 FT

On a perfect summer's day, the summit of High Stile is a place to linger: there is so much to see, such a feeling of well-being, it is so peaceful an environment, that the return to the world below is made with reluctance.

Two cairns a few yards apart occupy a rocky eminence immediately above the abrupt fall of rocks northwards and are magnificent viewpoints and are usually considered to mark the highest point although this is disputed by the Ordnance Survey triangulation station indicated by a large cairn nearby. The remains of a wire fence crosses the top and links with the neighbouring fells.

Paths leave the stony top for Red Pike and High Crag, that to the former descending roughly amongst boulders, that to High Crag being more gradual and soon levelling. Chapel Crags abut steeply on the summit at the head of Bleaberry Comb and constitute a danger for unwary walkers who stray from the beaten path.

Descents to Buttermere are usually made by way of Red Pike and the tourist path therefrom, although a scree gully in Chapel Crags offers a rough short cut to Bleaberry Tarn. A path also leaves Red Pike for High Gillerthwaite in Ennerdale. If returning to Buttermere by way of High Crag, it is perhaps safer to continue alongside the old fence down Gamlin End to join the Scarth Gap path; the upper exit of Sheepbone Rake may not be easy to locate from above and if missed this route is fraught with danger.

127

The Buttermere valley from High Stile

The prospect from the summit, especially looking north, has the hallmark of excellence. If viewpoints were awarded Oscars, this would be a popular nomination. In all directions the picture is of engrossing interest.

Across the gulf of Ennerdale, Great Gable and the Scafells are prominent and Pillar is directly opposite, its famous Rock seen frontally and its declining western ridge and foothills terminated by the full length of Ennerdale Water. More distantly, the Helvellyn and Skiddaw ranges are seen overtopping others. But the gem of the view, the scene that captivates by its colour and beauty, and by the depth of vision, is the perfect setting of the Buttermere valley in lovely surroundings far below and a resplendent Crummock Water encompassed by lofty heights. Rising steeply out of the valley and seen from tip to toe in comprehensive detail are the north-western fells, posing proudly as though for a family photograph: a view ranking amongst the best in Lakeland.

THE TRAVERSE OF THE RIDGE

The traverse of the ridge from end to end is a joyful exercise, the walk abounding in interesting situations and dramatic views. It is usually undertaken from Buttermere and better done clockwise so as to have the waterfall of Scale Force as a grand finale.

The ascent to High Crag should be made by way of Sheepbone Rake to avoid the tiring scree of Gamlin End. The summit of High Crag, 2443 ft is a fine viewpoint with a commanding view over the head of Ennerdale to Great Gable and the Scafells in particular. There is a large cairn decorated with iron posts from the dismantled fence alongside.

Crummock Water from Red Pike Below *Scale Force*

A short descent then follows to the narrow edge above Burtness Comb where, in a ring of crags, the precipice of Eagle Crag and the more broken rocks of Grey Crag are seen. Note here the splendid aerial view of Gatesgarth and the Honister Fells. An easy incline leads up to the summit of High Stile, the outlook north coming suddenly into sight in the course of the last few paces with stunning effect. It is difficult to tear oneself away from this wonderful scene but it must be done and the walk continued, roughly descending along the brink of Chapel Crags and then following the edge of Bleaberry Comb, less spectacular than Burtness Comb but having a tarn in its depths. A gentle rise brings the shapely summit of Red Pike underfoot. A large cairn, added to by visitors, adorns the top, 2479 ft.

The ridge is continued in the same direction along the edge of Ling Comb, above a scarp of crags, and when Scale Beck takes shape down on the left, a path slants across to it and descends alongside to the deep ravine containing the magnificent waterfall of Scale Force, plunging 100 feet in a single leap. This ends the ridge and a good pathway goes down to Crummock Water and Buttermere.

High Street

2718 ft

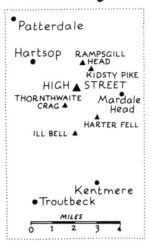

HIGH STREET IS IN stature the most massive of the fells on the far east of Lakeland, in altitude exceeding all the others in that company, and in strategic importance is the most influential, the summit being the apex of the longest ridge in the district and the central and culminating point of a complex pattern of valleys. Yet despite these credentials, High Street is unassuming and unpretentious and so accommodating to travellers that the Roman surveyors and engineers, during their early invasions of this country, laid a road across its broad top for the movement of troops and supplies in preference to their usual practice of seeking routes through the mountain passes. This ancient highway, still to be seen, gave High Street its unusual name.

Another unique distinction was earned much later, long after the departure of the Romans. A little community of farmers and shepherds developed at Mardale Green, and the inn, the Dun Bull, was the centre of social life, but every year a meeting of the dalesfolk took place on the top of High Street, and these were most convivial occasions. In addition to straying sheep being returned to their owners, a great feast was prepared, provisions and ale were brought up on the backs of horses, and sporting events arranged; chief among these was horse racing along the grassy sward that is such a feature of the top. In fact, the Ordnance maps of last century named the fell Racecourse Hill and only in more recent editions have they substituted the name High Street while retaining Racecourse Hill in small lettering.

High Street's bland and expressionless face to the west and the welcoming hospitality of its gentle upper slopes are not repeated on the east side, where the smooth summit breaks away suddenly in a chaotic fall of rocks to form a savage landscape – and it is this eastern aspect that most certainly measures up to my definition of a mountain. On the west, High Street is a hill; on the east it is a scene of alpine grandeur as though the veneer of grass had been stripped off by some contortion of nature long ago and the naked earth, lacking a protective cover, had been reduced by ages of weathering and erosion to an untidy debris of rocky ribs and arteries of stones.

Opposite *High Street from Kidsty Pike*

Hayeswater from the Roman road

The most prominent cliffs are Blea Water Crag, forming a rim along the edge of the summit and falling in disarray for a thousand feet down a steep fellside to a beautiful tarn, Blea Water. This occupies a deep hollow thought by some authorities to be the crater of an extinct volcano. The crags are broken into series but are not safe for exploration, two fatalities having occurred here; they are continued northwards into the head of Riggindale, interrupted only at one point where a tenuous ridge goes down to Rough Crag.

This is lonely country. There are few habitations in the valleys around and fewer still since the drowning of Mardale Green. Streams drain down into all the valleys, and reservoirs have been made above Low Hartsop and in Kentmere, but there is little cultivation, freedom from tourists, no commercial developments and a general inclination to let the region remain as nature fashioned it. But even a wilderness has supreme joys, and here, in the undisturbed solitude of the fells, are the grazing grounds of red deer, fell-ponies and sheep, contented and happy to be left in peace; there are the earths of foxes and the setts of badgers, while overhead the buzzards and the ravens and falcons keep watch, not now controlling the skies exclusively as of yore, golden eagles having joined their company. It is significant of the peace to be found in the High Street range, and the absence of man, that the eagles selected these lonely fells as their home on their return to this north-western corner of England.

Blea Water

132

The Roman road on High Street

THE ROMAN ROAD

Lakeland has been spared a turbulent history, the barren mountains being a deterrent to invaders and the marshy valleys offering little inducement to settlers until the Vikings and the Danes found it a home from home.

Before them, the Romans had been, not for pleasure or profit, but of necessity to reinforce their conquest of the country, building forts for their garrisons and linking them by roads to maintain communications. These roads did not linger: they went from A to B by the most direct route passable by men and supplies. The mountains were an obstacle, overcome by taking advantage of low passes. That is, in all cases but one: there was no easy way to link Galava (Ambleside) and Brocavum (Brougham) on a direct course and a road had to be made.

The Roman surveyors sent to reconnoitre a route found that High Street stood on the direct line between the two forts and must have been greatly relieved to find it relatively easy of access and that it presented no insuperable obstacles. The road was made. Between the two termini was a distance of twenty-seven Roman miles (twenty-five English) much of it over territory hitherto untrodden by man, and its maximum altitude of 2700 feet made it the highest road in the country, a distinction held for eighteen centuries until modern engineers built a motor road to the top of Great Dun Fell in the Pennines.

There were no problems during the first few miles: the road from Galava crossed via Skelghyll to the Troutbeck valley, high ground then being encountered in Hagg Gill, and ascended by a slanting groove, later known as Scot Rake after a skirmish between Scots and Brits at the time of the Border raids, so gaining the Ill Bell ridge near Thornthwaite Crag. Here, with the most arduous section behind, the road continued easily over the top of High Street and along the declining ridge to the north to valley level, near Brougham, there completing an early page in Lakeland's history.

Left *The pillar on Thornthwaite Crag*   Right *The Straits of Riggindale*

ASCENTS

The top of High Street is often reached during the course of a marathon walk along the main ridge but a variety of direct ascents, differing greatly in character, are available from Patterdale, Low Hartsop, Troutbeck, Kentmere and Mardale.

FROM PATTERDALE

It is a full day's expedition from Patterdale, there and back, following a route devised for travellers on ponies. Climbing steadily at first, a wide tract of open moorland is crossed to arrive on the main ridge at the Straits of Riggindale at the northern end of the mountain.

    The path, which is distinct throughout the journey, goes by way of Boardale Hause and Angle Tarn to reach open fell at Satura Crag where the main ridge comes into sight ahead, beyond an expanse of moorland, marshy in places: this is crossed, the path then rising to round the Knott, a conical hill, and then contours easily to reach a pronounced dip in the ridge – this is the Straits of Riggindale. Here a sudden stunning view of Mardale is revealed over the abyss of Riggindale: the highlight of the day's walk. The Roman Road or the broken wall, both coming down on the right, lead easily to the top of High Street: or, to keep the more exciting views of Mardale in sight, the rim of the eastern cliffs may be followed upwards until the Ordnance column on the summit is seen.

FROM LOW HARTSOP

This is the shorter of the two routes from the Kirkstone Pass road. The picturesque cluster of cottages at Low Hartsop, still with spinning galleries and steeped in the atmosphere of seventeenth-century Lakeland, has now been discovered by tourists and a car park provided for their use. Signs of former lead mining activity are passed as the walk starts along a good track alongside Hayeswater Gill, rising steadily into a profound hollow occupied by the large tarn of Hayeswater, now brought into service as a reservoir. Before reaching it, a path mounts the steep fellside of the Knott in a series of loops to ease the gradient and joins the path from Patterdale for the remainder of the walk.

Kentmere Reservoir

FROM TROUTBECK

This route substantially follows the line of the Roman Road.

From Troutbeck Town Head, the access road to Troutbeck Park Farm gives an easy start to Hagg Gill, where the slanting groove of Scot Rake leads upwards to the crest of the Ill Bell Ridge, there revealing a startling view down into Kentmere valley. The handsome pillar of stones on Thornthwaite Crag nearby is a compelling diversion before making the easy crossing to the top of High Street over a broad and featureless plateau of grass. On the flat summit, the highest point may be in doubt: it is marked by an Ordnance column, concealed on this approach by the broken ridge wall.

FROM KENTMERE

The Kentmere valley falls away directly from the southern slopes of High Street and would seem to offer a straightforward line of ascent. This it does but the climb out of the valley is steep, very rough and pathless, progress being made by trial and error in an undignified upward scramble: it is not a route to recommend to walkers who like to travel sedately.

A road continues up the west side of the valley beyond Kentmere Church to the last outpost of civilisation, Hartrigg Farm, and goes on into the upper recesses as a cart track, passing below the huge rock buttress of Rainsborrow Crag to an area of industrial decay. There are no silences more profound than those in places where men once laboured and are now deserted and abandoned and left to rot. Here are the quarries, spoil heaps and stone huts once vibrant with life, and over all is the silence of death. Further on, the path comes alongside Kentmere Reservoir, constructed to maintain supplies to fifteen water-powered mills along the banks of the River Kent. This too is out of commission and shares the general feeling of neglect. The spillway is still there and the river still issues, but the mills have gone and there is no use for it. There is sadness in upper Kentmere, a nineteenth-century industrial graveyard.

Ill Bell is the towering height above the reservoir and is succeeded by Froswick as the walk proceeds into the wild hollow ahead, from which the climb must be made without the help of a path or noteworthy landmarks: the choice of route is open. The best plan is to aim for Thornthwaite Crag where, after a great struggle, the ridge is joined for a final easy half-mile to the top of High Street.

FROM MARDALE

No other route of ascent can compare in interest and scenic quality with the direct climb out of Mardale. A curving ridge rising above the wooded promontory of the Rigg on Haweswater leads unerringly upwards to the summit plateau without deviation, the narrow crest giving grandstand views of the tremendous east face of the mountain. This is the connoisseur's way to the top of High Street.

A car park at the terminus of the Haweswater road at Mardale Head is the usual starting point. A path leads round the head of the reservoir and rises to a grassy saddle above the trees of the Rigg, a splendid viewpoint, the full length of Riggindale being here revealed. With a wall as guide, the ridge is ascended to a cairn on Rough Crag, the highest point of the narrowing crest, which calls for a protracted halt to survey the magnificent view in all directions. Behind is Harter Fell, looking its fiercest: down below on the left is Blea Water, snug in a hollow; over the wall to the right are the ramparts of the deep trench of Riggindale, across which is the shapely peak of Kidsty Pike. Looking forward, the mile-long escarpment of High Street is fully in view, Blea Water Crag being matched by the steep cliffs at the head of Riggindale. The route continues forward, descending to and crossing the grassy depression of Caspel Gate and then negotiating a steep and rocky rib to the easy grass on the summit.

Alternatively, and shorter, the path to Blea Water may be taken from Mardale Head, passing Dodderwick Force, and Caspel Gate is easily reached up a grassy slope; however, this route could never be preferred to the ridge of Rough Crag.

The Mardale route is an exhilarating approach to High Street, rich in rewards, and may even provide a bonus by the sight of a golden eagle in flight.

High Street from Mardale Head

136

Approaching the summit of High Street

THE SUMMIT: 2718 FT

The top of High Street forms a gentle curve a mile in length between the Kentmere edge and the Straits of Riggindale and, completely covered in grass, serves as a large pasture for sheep and a soft carpet for other fellwalkers. It totally lacks features of natural interest, the only furniture being a crumbled stone wall along the ridge from one end to the other and a column of the Ordnance Survey. But, although lacking in excitement, it can claim the distinction, not granted to other mountains, of having its Roman road, this running parallel to the wall.

One needs to be alone and blessed with imagination to fully appreciate High Street. Then in the mind's eye one can see the weary and dispirited legions of Roman soldiers on their long march, far from homes and families, strangers in a hostile land, thinking of themselves not as conquerors but as exiles from the sunny villages they had left behind. Or one can imagine the lively carousels of the dalesfolk at their annual meetings here in past centuries, the feastings, the wrestling, the horse racing and other sports, all combining to make the event their greatest day of the year. Or one can think of the men who built the stone wall two hundred years ago, finding their own material and sleeping on the site for pay of eightpence a day. Today, all these are forgotten men and only the mountain survives, now in perfect peace.

The Ordnance Survey column, like all such others, has become an antiquity, a thing of the past. No longer do the surveyors come on foot to make their triangulation readings from these columns. Photographs from aeroplanes and modern equipment give them the information they require with meticulous accuracy. A pity. These hoary columns were landmarks and old friends.

High Street is not as dull as first appearances suggest when approached along the ridge. No visit is complete without a deviation to the eastern edge of the summit plateau to look down on Blea Water in its wild setting and the rugged landscape of Mardale Head. Then High Street will get the respect it deserves.

High Street's superior elevation over neighbouring fells is emphasised by the comprehensive views from the summit, the distant prospect between south-west and north, although partly obstructed by the Helvellyn range, being particularly good. The Coniston fells, the Scafells, Great Gable and Pillar appear with many other familiar heights on the horizon. Skiddaw and Blencathra are seen to the north, and there is a glimpse of Windermere to the south with Morecambe Bay beyond. But there is no depth to the views because of the flat top around the Ordnance column: the valleys are hidden, and it is necessary to walk around the summit to reveal the more immediate surroundings. Especially not to be missed is the glorious outlook over Mardale from the top of Blea Water Crag: from this vantage point, the ground plunges a thousand feet to Blea Water in an embrace of bony arms, its issuing stream leading the eye down to the environs of Haweswater with Harter Fell a massive background to a wonderful scene. Those who can see no beauty in a wilderness should go and stand on the rim of Blea Water Crag.

THE HIGH STREET RIDGE

The ridge of which High Street is the focal point has its southern roots in the River Gowan near Ings, between Windermere and Staveley, and its northern in the valley of the River Eamont near Penrith. This is the longest continuous spine of high ground in lakeland and it has twelve vertebrae, such indicated by a separate fell summit. The twenty miles betweeen the extremities make the full traverse an endurance test for marathon walkers only: it is a long trek of diminishing pleasure and must be done, if at all, during the hours of daylight.

View from the top of Blea Water Crag

Upper Kentmere, from Thornthwaite Crag

Starting from High Borrans, north-west of Ings, the modest heights of Sour Howes, 1568 ft, and Sallows, 1691 ft, are climbed and a short descent made to the top of Garburn Pass: this is the only footpath across the ridge until Moor Divock is reached several hours later. Beyond the Pass, the ridge takes better shape and a wall guides the way to Yoke, 2309 ft, poised above an unseen Rainsborrow Crag and, directly ahead, is the conical Ill Bell, 2476 ft, with a multi-cairned summit and a fine retrospective view of Windermere. The prospect ahead is now much more exciting and steels the resolve to continue. A rough path goes down and then rises easily to Froswick, 2359 ft, a smaller imitation of Ill Bell, continuing then up a long slope to Thornthwaite Crag, 2569 ft.

Thus far the ridge has been the watershed between the valleys of Troutbeck and Kentmere, the one beautiful and pastoral, the other aggressively harsh and unfriendly in its upper reaches. There is now a simple crossing to the Roman road on High Street.

The Roman road can be trusted to lead safely over the top of High Street and down to the Straits of Riggindale, a pronounced gap in the ridge with a full-length view of Riggindale and Mardale beyond. From this point, walkers of faint heart who are beginning to think twice about the wisdom of continuing the marathon may take a path down to Patterdale, this being their only chance to escape from the ridge for several more miles.

The Roman road, which the route now follows closely, climbs up to Rampsgill Head, 2581 ft, leaving the shapely peak of Kidsty Pike away on the right; it then makes a beeline for High Raise, 2634 ft, the second highest summit on the ridge.

New landscapes appear. The lovely valley now down on the left is Martindale, for long the home of red deer, controlled but with freedom to roam. Half a mile to the right is the tumulus of Low Raise above a semi-circle of crags overlooking Haweswater.

From the stony top of High Raise, the ridge is seen continuing in a remarkably straight line and seemingly without end. Declining gradually and passing over minor bumps, the path, still based on the Roman road, reaches Wether Hill, 2210 ft, after a further two miles. The valley of Fusedale now appears below on the left, draining to Ullswater, and on the right, sprawling and undulating slopes extend over a wide territory of foothills before descending finally to Bampton and the valley of the River Lowther.

Still the ridge goes on and after another mile reaches the scanty ruins of Lowther House, in its heyday a shooting lodge, with stables. When I first came this way, the wooden structures had been dismantled and removed but a handsome stone fireplace and chimney stack remained in position: a surprising and unexpected landmark. Today there is nothing left intact. This ruin has the rounded top of Loadpot Hill, 2201 ft, as a background; the Romans decided to contour around the summit.

The ruins of Lowther House

The stone circle on Moor Divock

Loadpot Hill is the last major height on the marathon, and here the ridge is much wider. Easy slopes descend to the left, culminating in the summits of Bonscale Pike and Arthur's Pike before plunging steeply to Ullswater; and on the right a slowly declining upland, a haunt of fell-ponies, goes down into Heltondale. The outlook ahead from Loadpot Hill looks friendlier, encouraging the hope that the long walk is coming to an end. Not yet, however. The Roman road is rejoined and leads gently downhill with an increasing promise of valley comforts soon to come. The green depression of Moor Divock, with its bridleways and footpaths to places of refreshment, is now the objective but three more miles must be trodden before it is reached at a place that must have caused the Romans some surprise. Their road comes alongside a large circle of stones arranged and later abandoned by primitive men thousands of years earlier, with other evidences of prehistoric occupation nearby. This circle is named The Cockpit on Ordnance maps.

On Moor Divock, the character of the scenery changes, a welcome transition to limestone after the acid peat of the journey thus far, and this makes the conditions underfoot more pleasant. The Roman road beyond the stone circle is very distinct, possibly because of its use by pony trekkers.

The purists will feel an obligation to climb Heughscar Hill from Moor Divock as the logical end of the ridge: others less troubled by conscience will call it a day and go down to Pooley Bridge. Heughscar Hill, 1231 ft, which has a superb view of Ullswater, is an easy climb amongst limestone outcrops.

Here we say goodbye to the Roman road, which skirts the hill; and to the longest ridge in Lakeland.

Hopegill Head

2525 ft

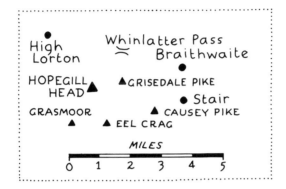

THE HIGH RIDGE SPRINGING suddenly out of Braithwaite carries a well-worn path to Grisedale Pike and continues westwards to end equally abruptly above Crummock Water. Midway along it is a sharp peak which, in the absence of clear definition on early maps, became known to generations of walkers as Hobcarton Pike, and still is – although the Ordnance Survey has now decreed that it should be named Hopegill Head. It is not quite the highest point on the ridge, Grisedale Pike having that honour, but undoubtedly the finest and it is surprising that so little attention has been paid to it in the past with only an occasional brief mention in guide books. I think myself that Hobcarton Pike is the more appropriate name but there is topographical justification for the official name given to it by the Ordnance Survey and Hopegill Head must be accepted.

The outstanding feature of the mountain, an awesome spectacle of massed rock formations on a grand scale, is the dark crescent of Hobcarton Crag, its grim impressiveness accentuated by perpetual shadow, with cliffs falling immediately from the slender summit and supporting ridges, the whole presenting a scene of natural grandeur unsurpassed in this region of Lakeland. Hobcarton Crag is monstrous and repelling, yet even in the gloomy recesses there is beauty and colour. The black rocks are interspersed by terraces of lush green vegetation and hanging gardens of bilberry while for intrepid botanists there is the thrill of locating *Viscaria alpina*, the red alpine catchfly, in its only known English habitat.

Scooped out of the mountain is the deep trench of the Hobcarton valley, descending from the crags to the conifer plantations of Whinlatter.

The main ridge goes on beyond Hopegill Head on an undulating course to Whiteside, bounded on one side by Gasgale and on the other by the Vale of Lorton in a contrast of utter wildness and verdant loveliness. The mountain has only one easy line of approach, by way of Coledale Hause, passing over the grassy mount of Sand Hill, which the early cartographers named more prominently on their maps than the summit. All streams are destined for the River Cocker and there are no tarns.

Opposite Hopegill Head from Ladyside Pike

ASCENTS

Unlike the neighbouring summits of Grisedale Pike and Whiteside, which are invariably reached by climbing the extremities of the ridge, Hopegill Head may be approached from all four points of the compass, emphasising its role as the hub of this group of fells.

FROM BRAITHWAITE VIA GRISEDALE PIKE

The popular path leaving the Whinlatter road at Braithwaite climbs steeply, with an easier middle section but has little of interest, apart from glorious restrospective views, until the summit is reached. Then the tremendous facade of Hopegill Head appears suddenly and with startling effect. The ridge descends towards this imposing scene, reaching a depression from which, in an atmosphere of high drama, the rising edge of Hobcarton Crag is followed up to the neat summit of Hopegill Head.

FROM BRAITHWAITE VIA COLEDALE HAUSE

A less arduous route from Braithwaite, omitting Grisedale Pike, takes advantage of the mine road along Coledale and continues as a rising path to Coledale Hause. Here Hopegill Head tops the easy but pathless grass slopes on the right, the summit remaining concealed until the subsidiary Sand Hill is crossed; then it comes into sight at close range and is only five exciting minutes away. This moment of revelation is the one highlight of a rather tedious walk. Or, from the Hause, a beeline may be made to the depression on the ridge below Grisedale Pike, avoiding old mine workings on the way, there to share with walkers who have come over the Pike the thrilling climb along the edge of Hobcarton Crag.

Hopegill Head from Whiteside

Hopegill Head from Hope Gill

FROM LANTHWAITE VIA WHITESIDE

The path to Whiteside leaves the entrance to Gasgale Gill and climbs to the minor elevation of Whin Ben, continuing thence up heathery slopes to the top. An enjoyable traverse of the undulating ridge extending eastwards, with sensational views down to Gasgale Gill, leads to the cairn on Hopegill Head. Alternatively from Lanthwaite but not to be preferred, Gasgale Gill may be followed up to Coledale Hause for a direct ascent over Sand Hill.

FROM HOPEBECK VIA HOPE GILL

An unorthodox and unfrequented route, with restricted views but the merit of directness, leaves the old waggonette road north of The Hope and comes alongside the descending stream of Hope Beck. It is surprising to have the benefit of a good path in such lonely terrain, the reason being explained when it ends at a sheepfold as the walk proceeds upstream. As the fellsides converge more steeply, Hope Beck becomes Hope Gill and now it is plain to see why Hopegill Head is so named, the mountain towering directly above the source of the stream. The best plan here is to strike half-left to gain the north ridge coming over Ladyside Pike and follow this upwards, Hobcarton Crag being seen in its full immensity to provide a spectacular finish to the walk. Just before the final summit pyramid, the ridge is cut into by a great gash, which I call the Notch, rocky pavements nearby adding further interest. The summit cairn is reached along a weakness in the uppermost stage of the climb.

The Summit: 2525 ft

The summit is a delightful place for a halt, a rocky upthrust of delicate proportions contrasting with the sprawling expanses round about. A cairn poised above the abyss of Hobcarton Crag has a commanding outlook over all lines of approach.

The view is constricted in the south by the greater nearby heights of Eel Crag and Grasmoor and only to the west across the Solway Firth is there an unobstructed distant prospect. Eastwards, the skyline is formed by the entire Helvellyn range but generally is not comprehensive. Crummock Water is the only lake in the picture.

I remember arriving on the summit one sunny day and finding a noisy commotion in progress: the stones of the cairn were plastered with flying ants, the prey of about thirty swifts wheeling and darting around, so obsessed by this rare feast that they were quite oblivious of my presence, indeed passed within my reach. The cairn was under siege. This was the only occasion when I have been within a few feet of a summit cairn yet failed to touch it.

GRISEDALE PIKE

Grisedale Pike is the conspicuous object in view from Braithwaite, its shapely soaring dome presenting a challenge that cannot be ignored or resisted. There is only one feasible route to the top, by a much-travelled path climbing the fellside from the Whinlatter road and finally mounting a rough ridge to the summit. The flank bounding Coledale is too steep for a direct ascent. The name derives from a valley descending north, one of the three Grisedales in Lakeland: its lower reaches are masked by conifer plantations.

The best reward for the ascent of Grisedale Pike, 2593 ft, is the beautiful view of the Vale of Keswick with peeps of Bassenthwaite Lake and Derwentwater, and in all directions except south the prospect is far reaching. The Cumbrian coast is seen without interruption.

WHITESIDE

Whiteside terminates the ridge in the south and here too there is only one route of ascent served by a continuous path, as described on page 145. Although pathless, exploratory ascents may be made from the Vale of Lorton without hindrance. An easy ridge connects with Hopegill Head, providing dramatic views down into Gasgale: this slope is extremely rough and is terraced by crags.

The view from the cairn at 2317 ft is rather circumscribed by higher fells, and the expected outlook over Crummock Water and Loweswater does not materialise until a short stroll west brings them into the picture.

Left *The ridge looking towards Whiteside*
Opposite *Whiteside*

Langdale Pikes

2403 ft

ONCE SEEN, NEVER FORGOTTEN. Other places may slip from the memory but the distinctive profile of the Langdale Pikes, once seen, leaves an indelible imprint on the mind. They are instantly recognisable not only by walkers and climbers but also by other visitors to the district who normally take little interest in identifying mountains and even less in ascending them. Whenever they appear in a view, they arrest attention. They are highly magnetic, constantly drawing the eyes and compelling the feet. To artists and photographers they are irresistible, yet their appeal comes not from grace or beauty, which they lack. They look down on the valley of Great Langdale like a pride of crouching lions: they look fierce, hostile, repelling, yet they are greatly loved by devotees who return time after time as pilgrims to a shrine and at all seasons of the year for another friendly wrestle with the giants of the group. And their conquests are happy occasions to think about in exile. All days spent on the Langdale Pikes are golden days.

It is not a superior elevation that so distinguishes the Pikes from all others: indeed there are greater heights nearby which have every right to feel sullen and resentful at the greater attention given to their lesser neighbours. But let nobody dare to call the Pikes hills. They are proud mountains in their own right, every inch, and demand to be treated with the respect they deserve.

There are five distinct summits in the group, all within a mile in distance, yet not crowded together. Each has individual characteristics, being alike only in their very steep fall to the valley floor, their sides buttressed by crags and split by drainage gullies bringing streams down from the upper ramparts to join Great Langdale Beck and ultimately Windermere. These slopes soar two thousand feet in a lateral distance of less than half a mile and their ascent is a battle against gravity, a treadmill with the toil greatly relieved by scenic gems, imposing rock architecture and fascinating occurrences along the way, while the frequent necessary halts are regaled by lovely views of the green strath of the valley pastures below. In terrain so rugged and uncompromising, it is not surprising that only one path in regular use has been forged to the skyline above and that most walkers adhere to it strictly and do not attempt to deviate. But it is a stairway to heaven.

Opposite *Langdale Pikes from Side Pike*

Langdale Pikes from the north

The five summits are, from the west: Pike o'Stickle, Loft Crag, Thorn Crag, Harrison Stickle and Pavey Ark, each of them having well-defined boundaries and claiming sovereignty over its own affairs, yet on nodding terms with its neighbours. Each too has natural features peculiar to itself and cannot be confused with the others. They are individuals, not quintuplets. All combine however, to give walkers who attain the ridge a delightful tour of changing vistas and recurring surprises as their reward for the effort of getting there, all contributing to make the short journey, calling on each in turn, one of the finest miles in Lakeland. Nor is the passage from one to the other at all arduous, the hard work of the day being over when the ridge is reached. To be aloft up here with a few hours to spare is a joy known only to fellwalkers.

The five Pikes, although different in structure, do share in common the steepness and severity of the slopes descending to Great Langdale from their stark and angular skyline, leading to an expectation that the summit ridge will be found to be narrow and tenuous and succeeded immediately by similar steep declivities on the northern flank of the group. But this is not so. On a first visit, walkers who attain the ridge without consulting a map are astonished to discover that an extensive and uninteresting moorland continues north from the ridge at an elevation only little lower. From this side the Pikes are revealed as imposters, insignificant undulations along the edge of a dreary plateau. The contrast is absolute. The Pikes exhibit a bold front exclusively to Great Langdale. They are mountains with one side only. That one side, however, has more than enough to delight every fellwalker who sets foot on it. It is the Pikes' well-stocked shop window, full of good things. But the shop behind is empty.

Pike o'Stickle from Loft Crag

PIKE O'STICKLE

It seems a fair conjecture that Pike o'Stickle's name derives from its close relationship with Harrison Stickle, being earlier regarded as a pike or peak of the parent mountain, and indeed it is the only one in the group sufficiently sharply pointed to deserve such recognition although all are now known collectively as the Langdale Pikes.

Pike o'Stickle is certainly the shapeliest of the group, the only one with pretensions to grace of outline and a pointed top. From all directions it has the appearance of a tapering dome, even from the north where the summit superstructure of 2323 ft is all that can be seen. Simplicity of design is another attribute that distinguishes the Pike from its fellows. A glance is enough for full appreciation: there are no ridges, no ramifications, no secret recesses. The Pike puts all its cards on the table: nothing is hidden from the sight of an observer. There is a feline smoothness and sleekness not usually associated with mountain structures but these are not weaknesses: on the contrary, the great unbroken sweep of the southern front, Stickle Breast, as it springs from the side valley of Mickleden is quite unrelenting through a height of nearly two thousand feet, narrowing as it rises in tiers of crags to the thimble-like top between two gullies defining its boundaries. Sleek it may be, but it is not to be stroked.

Direct ascents are out of the question. The summit is usually approached from the Harrison Stickle path when the ridge is reached, or less frequently by a forgotten drove road alongside Troughton Beck out of Mickleden. The end more than justifies the means.

The summit of Pike o'Stickle looking to Harrison Stickle

THE STONE AXE FACTORY

The chance discovery by a Kendal fellwalker of a stone axehead amongst the screes in one of the gullies of Pike o'Stickle in the early years after the last war and the subsequent finding of many more brought the Pike into the national limelight, at least in archaeological and antiquarian circles. Some of the finds were perfect specimens, handmade by chipping, but most had defects and had apparently been rejected and thrown aside by their makers. Investigations led to the conclusion, now established beyond doubt, that the axes were the work of Neolithic men thousands of years before the recording of history, and geological surveys proved that the stone used for making the implements came from a narrow vein of very hard rock which was alien to the volcanic deposits prevailing in the area and was continuous along a high contour around the valley. Chipping sites have been found nearby, notably on Martcrag Moor and Harrison Stickle. It was an important industry, possibly even with an export trade, other specimens from Great Langdale having been found in other parts of the country.

What really beggars the imagination is not so much the presence of this particular strata of rock, nor the making of implements from it so long ago, but that the primitive inhabitants of Lakeland should have located such an insignificant geological fault two thousand feet up a wild fellside and recognised its value; and that the plentiful evidences of their industry should have remained undisturbed and unnoticed throughout the ages until recent times.

A man-made cave hewn out of the rock wall near the top of the gully, a few feet square and large enough to shelter several persons, seems to have been connected with the manufacture of the axes, a theory not yet accepted by expert opinion although the coincidence seems too obvious to be denied.

LOFT CRAG

Next in line to Pike o'Stickle along the skyline ridge is the pleasant summit of Loft Crag, at 2270 ft a comfortable throne overlooking a kingdom of scenic splendour and providing grassy couches that invite a siesta: sleepwalkers, however, should not tarry long since the top soon breaks into lethal crags on the Langdale side. Indeed, Loft Crag has the most formidable build-up of rocks in the group, Pavey Ark excepted; an upper fringe drops sharply to the huge near-vertical tower of Gimmer Crag, a top favourite amongst rock-climbers. Gimmer Crag is almost severed from the fellside by a deep cleft but admits no further weakness; it forms a formidable three-sided tower with a network of very testing routes pioneered by enthusiasts and often festooned with their ropes.

Northwards from the summit and totally different is a high and featureless tableland of interest only to sheep.

The summit is invariably reached and then left along the ridge, direct ascents and descents being suicidal.

Right *Gimmer Crag*
Below *Loft Crag from Pike o'Stickle*

THORN CRAG

At 2120ft Thorn Crag is the least assertive and aggressive of the Pikes and hardly merits inclusion in their august company, its relative insignificance and absence of hazards leading to its selection as the easiest route by which the pedestrian path can reach the ridge. This path, well cairned, climbs the west slope avoiding frontal roughnesses, and curves round the back. It is grass all the way, and from it the summit can be visited by a very simple detour, being found to be merely a gentle mound. In fact, Thorn Crag may be said to have no back side at all; the ground declining imperceptibly into the hollow of Harrison Combe whence it appears only as a slight swelling on the ridge.

But the eastern side is a very different story. Here the summit is bordered by steep ground, with cliffs falling almost precipitously into a deep ravine of immense proportions, a great rift difficult to explain. The infant Dungeon Ghyll flows through it but is merely a trickle coming from a restricted gathering ground and certainly has never had the force and momentum to carve such a channel: it must therefore be ascribed to a convulsion of nature when the landscape was formed millions of years ago.

This ravine often escapes notice. The path to Harrison Stickle leaves Thorn Crag and fords the stream in Harrison Combe before it enters the ravine, and the many walkers who tread the path usually have their attention concentrated on the final stage of the climb and have no interest in the further progress of the stream and miss seeing a remarkable manifestation of nature's primeval sculpturing.

The upper ravine of Dungeon Ghyll

Dungeon Ghyll

The upper waterfall

DUNGEON GHYLL

Ghyll is a fanciful version of *gill*, the Norse word for a mountain stream or a narrow ravine, adopted in the more romantic times when the writings of the Lake Poets brought the district into national prominence and gave a degree of sophistication to the places first visited by the early Victorian tourists. The new spelling of the name was applied mainly in the more accessible southern part of Lakeland, the most notable examples being Dungeon Ghyll in Langdale and Stock Ghyll in Ambleside. Jenkinson's guide in the mid-nineteenth century would have none of it, but the hotels in Great Langdale followed suit and the new name is now firmly established.

Dungeon Ghyll is the principal stream coming down from the Langdale Pikes and its popular waterfall, Dungeon Ghyll Force, is usually considered the highlight of the ascent. Everybody halts here and many go no further. The Force is in an attractive setting in a deep gorge but is not easily seen when partly hidden by summer foliage on the trees lining the gorge. The path is directly alongside and soon turns left to continue the ascent, leaving the stream which comes down a rough defile on the right. This defile has chokes of boulders and progress along it without the help of a path is rather arduous but, on turning a corner, a delightful scene is revealed: a slender waterfall plunges in an unbroken leap of fifty feet into a rocky basin from which it escapes through a breach in the edge to form a second fall. This higher waterfall is well away from the paths of tourists and seldom seen, yet to my mind is much finer than the over-publicised Force. Escape from the defile is by a scrambling exit on the left of the fall, emerging on a grassy prairie bisected by the descending stream, now docile, which can then be followed up to the ravine below Thorn Crag. Beyond here, the path to Harrison Stickle can be rejoined, the whole route thus giving an alternative line of ascent.

Harrison Stickle from Pike How   *Top of Stickle Gill*

HARRISON STICKLE

I never discovered who Harrison was but presume it to be the name of a Langdale man who, in the forgotten past, either owned or grazed his sheep upon the mountain long known as Harrison Stickle. The absence of such knowledge, however, does not detract from its majestic presence nor the excellence of the climb to its rocky top at 2403 ft.

Harrison Stickle is the undisputed overlord of the Langdale Pikes. In height, bulk and in importance, it surpasses the others in the group; the kingpin, the boss, a cock amongst hens, not asking the lesser members of the family to bow and scrape for they too have their pride, but undisputably superior in every way. The top is a dark tower of rock, the object that most attracts the eyes of visitors coming up Great Langdale; indeed, seeming to timid observers to threaten the valley. Below this tower is a brief easing of gradient and then a final plunge to the little community of Dungeon Ghyll where all fierceness is spent and harshness mellowed in a rural environment of trees and green pastures.

The southern boundaries of the mountain are clearly defined by the watercourses of Dungeon Ghyll and Mill Gill, but to the north defy definition in the marshy hollow of Harrison Combe.

ASCENTS

When walkers talk of climbing the Langdale Pikes, it is Harrison Stickle they invariably have in mind and the route they follow is almost certainly the well-worn path that visits Dungeon Ghyll Force and then rises in twists and bends to an easier upper plateau, where a branch goes off to Gimmer Crag, and then goes on to mount and round Thorn Crag. Here the path renews acquaintance with Dungeon Ghyll, at this point in the innocence of infancy, and finally climbs the last slope to the summit.

The more direct route, keeping alongside Dungeon Ghyll throughout, is another possibility but it is pathless and will not suit all tastes. The shortest and best, although not in favour, takes a higher path from the valley to arrive at the neat little summit of Pike How and then, with a track underfoot, heads up a grassy incline to pass above the upper ravine near a stone-axe chipping site to join the tourist path before the final rise to the summit. This way is quiet and greatly to be recommended on days of chattering crowds.

An overused path, trampled to death by clumsy boots, climbs alongside Mill Gill – which the Ordnance Survey have now re-christened Stickle Gill – en route for Stickle Tarn and Pavey Ark but may also be adopted for an ascent of Harrison Stickle. This path, on the west bank of the stream, has been sadly abused. As long as forty years ago, when I often came this way, it was degenerating into an unpleasant scree run and I always preferred to use the east bank although, at that time, it was not furnished with a path. Since then the condition of the west path has become so bad and even dangerous that the wardens have shown their concern by repairing sections of it and closing others, deflecting walkers to the east bank which, in turn, may suffer the same fate.

At the top of the east bank Tarn Crag, an area of rocky slabs easy to negotiate, and immediately beyond is Stickle Tarn, a large expanse of water below the crags of Pavey Ark: a dramatic scene, one I believe to be the most impressive in the Langdales. A dam proclaims the former use of the tarn as a reservoir, when it served the gunpowder works at Elterwater. From this point, a steep grassy slope on the left can be climbed to a ridge above; here rocky steps lead to the summit of Harrison Stickle.

Stickle Tarn

THE SUMMIT OF HARRISON STICKLE

The summit of Harrison Stickle is an elevated rock platform, the cairn crowning the northern end of a short ridge. This is thinly covered by a veneer of turf scraped away by boots in many places to reveal the underlying solid plinth of rock. North of the cairn, the ground breaks away in a bouldery stairway going down to the col and a ridge gently rises to the top of Pavey Ark: this and the path coming up from Thorn Crag are the only safe ways off the summit which is elsewhere circumscribed by crags. The Thorn Crag path arrives at the south cairn seventy yards from the main highest point, and here most visitors linger to appraise the sensational aerial view of the valley from the brink of the precipitous cliffs buttressing the summit.

   The view from Harrison Stickle more than repays the effort of the climb. It is wonderfully diverse, crammed with detail in every direction except westwards where Bowfell obscures the distance and the Wasdale giants merely peep over a high horizon. It is to the east and south that the view really excels, the whole of the Helvellyn range and the beautiful environs of Windermere being fully revealed. This is a prospect that profits from the abrupt fall around the summit, giving unusual depth to the landscapes.

View south from Harrison Stickle

Pavey Ark and Stickle Tarn from Harrison Stickle

PAVEY ARK

Pavey Ark, 2288 ft high, is the grandest and most imposing cliff in the Langdale area, a colossus of rock of gigantic proportions, an awesome precipice that always staggers the senses no matter how often it is visited. In alliance with Stickle Tarn which bathes the feet of this monstrous giant the scene they present, while having nothing of beauty, has no equal in Lakeland: an awesome, almost brutal composition fashioned by nature and unchanged since the beginning of time. When this picture is suddenly revealed at the top of the usual path from the valley, the effect is electrifying.

Pavey Ark is set back from the other Pikes and does not obtrude in the Langdale landscape as they do, nor has it their thrusting aggression. Of retiring disposition and remaining aloof, the Ark has a majesty and dignity the others lack; it is best appreciated when the day's visitors have departed and the great wall of rock is gripped in a deathly silence. Then the scene is overpowering.

Pavey Ark was in at the birth of rock-climbing. A hundred years ago it was the toast of the early pioneers who practised their sport in the cavernous gullies and chimneys of the crag with ropes only: the pitons and karabiners of modern climbers were unheard of and I doubt whether those adventurous Victorians would have approved their use. Attitudes and techniques have changed since those early days and Gimmer Crag has usurped the Ark in the affections of Langdale rock-climbers. It is always sad when a proud reputation is diminished by extraneous events and, although still the subject of much attention and new discoveries in route finding, Pavey Ark has lost its superiority: that is, in the esteem of climbers. It may be old-fashioned, but to the rest of us this ancient pile of rocks remains supreme. The tears it sheds drain into Stickle Tarn and are carried away to be submerged and lost in Windermere.

The summit of Pavey Ark is easily attained along a ridge from Harrison Stickle or by climbing the grassy slope above the dam of Stickle Tarn, or from the wide moorland behind, and it is by one or other of these routes that most pedestrians reach the top cairn.

But to red-blooded walkers, these expedients amount to cheating. Is it not possible to find a way up the tremendous 500-feet wall of rock and survive the attempt? Well yes, there is a way, just one.

Opposite *The first section of Jack's Rake*   Above *Pavey Ark from Stickle Tarn*

JACK'S RAKE

There is no positive identification of Jack and it must be assumed that he was a Langdale shepherd who wanted to get from the bottom of the crag to the top without going all the way round. He found such a way and earned immortality by doing so. The route he discovered will forever be known as Jack's Rake.

From a recess at the foot of East Buttress, a narrow groove, safely secured by a rock parapet, goes up very steeply to the left: this is the first section of the Rake and long legs are a hindrance in the tight confines of the groove. Then follows a simple terrace with an unprotected edge above a vertical drop; next is another groove and then the chasm of Great Gully is crossed to broken rocks and a final scramble to the top.

Jack's Rake has become a very popular test for fellwalkers and through overuse is reported to be eroded and slippery on the terrace: much care should be taken. It is gratifying, having done it, to note that the Rake is classed as a rock climb (admittedly the easiest of the easy) in the rock-climbing guides. It is the only notch in my belt and there will be no more.

EASY GULLY

Another route to the top also leaving the recess on an opposite tangent is provided by Easy Gully which, except for a huge and awkward chockstone, has no serious difficulties. It joins a steep and narrow grass slope, which I call the North Rake, up which the summit cairn may be reached without further problems.

The North Rake and Easy Gully are suitable for descent; Jack's Rake is not.

Pillar

2927 ft

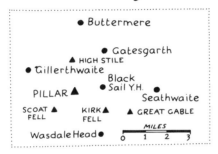

WHEN I WAS A young man my visits to the Lake District were of necessity restricted to day excursions on the train to Windermere and, in due course, I became very familiar with the glorious countryside within a ten-mile radius of the railway station. I longed to be able to get further afield. Studying the Ordnance Survey map of the district was a daily ritual for me over many years: I knew the details by heart although most of the region remained out of reach. I pinpointed all the mountains on the map, these having an exciting attraction for me: we had valleys and hills at home but no mountains. In particular, two mountain names fired my imagination: in the western fells were Pillar and Steeple, and for twenty years they plagued my mind until I was able to see and set foot on them. Even when I moved to Kendal, thereby bringing all the mountains within closer range, wartime restrictions on travel kept me in exile. At last the chance came for a visit to Wasdale Head and I set forth eagerly to realise a long ambition and see the promised pinnacles.

They were disappointing. Pillar was nothing like a pillar and Steeple bore only a slight resemblance to a steeple. But the area of which they formed part was a revelation, an assembly of bare rocky peaks in a wilderness landscape very different from the lush greenery of the environs of Windermere: here was loneliness and solitude and an array of silent but challenging mountains. Pillar and Steeple had not the expected needle-sharp spires but they were wonderful members of a wonderful company.

I had known in advance that Pillar took its name from a famous rock on the Ennerdale side of the mountain: in fact, I was so steeped in the publications of the Fell and Rock Climbing Club and the excellent photographs of the Abraham brothers (which latter have never been equalled) that I had long formed a mental picture of Pillar Rock in detail. Even so, the reality greatly exceeded expectations. First sight of it was breathtaking.

Pillar Rock is different. Unlike most of the climbing grounds in the district it is not part of a cliff or crag but an independent column of rock thrust out of the fellside in a near-vertical leap of 600 feet from tip to toe. The Rock, despite its lonely situation remote from habitations, had a local fame and notoriety long before the invasion of tourists; it was first climbed by a shepherd in 1828, a feat hitherto regarded as impossible. Today it is Number One objective for rock-climbers but in succumbing to their efforts has lost nothing of its majesty and dignity.

Opposite *Pillar from Green How*

Pillar is essentially masculine, all sinew and muscle, but has been shamefully forced, without option, to wear dark green skirts on the lower Ennerdale slopes and, even more offensive, they are clothes of foreign origin, and unsightly. A million wretched conifers, densely crowded together and fighting for light to ease their misery, stand like an army of skeletons with withered and lifeless limbs; they cover the valley floor in a shroud, hiding the little that remains of its native beauty. Every tree starts life determined to grow into a noble specimen but here in Ennerdale they never have a chance: they are born to be telegraph poles. This is battery forestry with no compassion or feeling for its victims.

I remember climbing Pillar from Ennerdale when the valley was open to the sky and bare of trees, and when the only sounds were the music of the beautiful river and the croaking of frogs in the mosses. It was so much better then. The proposal to blanket Ennerdale with alien conifers met with little opposition at the time: conservationists were thin on the ground in those days and their voice was ineffective. The events in Ennerdale are unhappily symptomatic of other unwelcome developments in the district. There are too many Big Brothers in the Lakeland scene.

Another culprit is the Tourist Board whose continuous exhortations to the public to visit the Lake District have robbed the valleys and villages of their former unique charms; they are now crowded with cars, caravans and coaches which have brought an infestation of tourists and rubbernecks many of whom have no eye for the natural beauty around and find their main interest in cafes and gift shops. Thank goodness these misguided authorities have not yet cast their sights on the mountains. I fear they will and that future generations of fellwalkers may have to do battle with chairlifts on Helvellyn, leisure centres with all the fun of the fair in places like Sty Head and cheap souvenir shops on the passes. Lakeland is not the earthly paradise it was when I was a lad. It has become horribly commercial.

Having got that off my chest let us return to Pillar, a fine bold mountain overtopping all else around and forming a high barrier between the valleys of Ennerdale and Mosedale; the latter is a deep trench that has not suffered the intrusion of man and is a sanctuary furnished as nature intended. Pillar has a long ridge eastwards descending in stages to Black Sail Pass and a shorter one westwards that overlooks the wild recess of Windgap Cove before losing itself under a canopy of conifers. Streams from Pillar aim for Wastwater and Ennerdale Water, and there are no tarns.

ASCENTS

Pillar is most often climbed from Wasdale Head by way of Gatherstone Beck and Black Sail Pass, the east ridge being reached at Looking Stead and followed up alongside the remains of a wire fence to the flat top of the mountain.

An alternative route from Wasdale Head, more direct but less popular, persists along Mosedale and at the head of the valley climbs very steeply on a path that has degenerated into an unpleasant scree run to Wind Gap, from which the summit is soon reached up a rocky slope.

From the Black Sail Youth Hostel at the head of Ennerdale, beyond the plantations, a path climbs to the top of Black Sail Pass where the east ridge can be joined and followed over Looking Stead to the top.

From mid-Ennerdale, the River Liza is crossed by a footbridge and a path followed through a firebreak in the forest to emerge in Windgap Cove; here either the rough west ridge may be followed upwards alongside a line of fence posts or, more usual, the Cove ascended to Wind Gap in impressive surroundings. This approach is the best of all.

Above *Windgap Cove from Ennerdale*   Below *Summit ridge at Windgap Cove*

Above *Robinson's Cairn from the High Level Traverse*　Opposite *Pillar Rock*

THE HIGH LEVEL TRAVERSE

The early climbers on Pillar Rock devised a short cut from their base at Wasdale Head that lead directly to the Rock from the east ridge and saved themselves the effort of first climbing to the summit of the mountain before getting to grips with their objective.

They named this short cut the High Level Traverse, and later generations of walkers and climbers have good reason to be grateful for their ingenuity since their path offers an easy and pleasant walk and maintains a high contour across a hostile fellside to reveal, suddenly and with startling effect, the awesome profile of the Rock directly ahead. It is a dramatic sight that transfixes the eyes to the exclusion of all else and stops allcomers in their tracks. In that moment a memory is born and will never die.

The High Level route branches from the east ridge at the foot of the first rise beyond Looking Stead. At the time of my first visit, the point of departure from the ridge path was not clear and it was necessary to move gingerly along a horizontal crack in the face of a crag to gain the new path beyond; on a later occasion I found that the crag had been avoided by a descent and re-ascent, and with this initial difficulty removed, there are now no problems on the route, which goes straight forward below the rising ridge, on the left forming a series of rock buttresses, and with Ennerdale far below on the right. The instant revelation comes upon topping a small eminence crowned by Robinson's Cairn.

Walkers' attention will be drawn to a tablet which is fixed to a rock near the cairn. This is a memorial to John Wilson Robinson who was a fellwalker in the early days who had seemingly endless energy. It is said that he often walked from where he lived in Lorton over the Scarth Gap and Black Sail Passes to Wasdale Head where he would accompany his friends for a day's rock-climbing. Then he walked all the way home again. Do read the beautiful words on the memorial tablet before you pass by.

High Man, Pillar Rock

PILLAR ROCK

Pillar Rock has been likened to a shattered cathedral but the simile is not only as regards its imposing structure: the Rock is twice the height of most cathedrals and far from being shattered is very firmly rooted in the fellside. This is no crumbling edifice but an immense tower of solid and immovable rock, nature's architecture on a massive scale and constructed to a master design.

In essence, Pillar Rock is one tower superimposed on another. From the base, a sheer wall soars upwards almost vertically for 400 feet to halt for a breather at a commodious ledge bearing a cairn; this section is known as Low Man. Then after this brief respite the wall resumes its upward flight to come to rest finally on the top of the Rock, and the upper super-structure is called the High Man. The Rock is cut away from the fellside at High Man by a deep cleft and on both sides is severed from adjoining ground by gullies: thus it is a separate entity within clearly defined boundaries. Seen from the east, however, its isolation is not apparent since the dividing gully is hidden by a flanking cliff that seems to be part of the main mass; because of this deception, it has the name of Shamrock.

After a century and a half of exploration, Pillar Rock has yielded to the rock-climbing fraternity a wide variety of routes of ascent of all degrees of difficulty, those on the north front of Low Man and the west side of High Man in particular being of exceptional severity. To a non-climbing observer whose feet are firmly planted on easy ground nearby, the human flies inching their way up the precipitous walls of rock seem to be performing the impossible. Pillar Rock is for very brave men only.

From Robinson's Cairn a short foray up the stony fellside leads to a rising shelf, the Shamrock Traverse, that gives an easy passage above the Shamrock and comes face to face with High Man at close range in an area littered with rock debris and boulders; a sensational confrontation. In view at this point, amongst a network of climbing routes, is the only easy way to the top of High Man (easy, that is, according to rock-climbing classification), the Slab and Notch Route. It has been a long-time ambition of mine, never satisfied, to stand on the top of High Man, and on several occasions I have made my way to the Slab and Notch determined to conquer it, but it never looked easy to me. Legs turned to jelly and resolve withered. I find consolation for failure in that I have kept alive and accident-free for over eighty years. There was formerly a stretcherbox sited at the end of the Traverse to cater for climbing casualties but this was removed to the base of the Rock some years ago, a decision that made sense because, in compliance to Newton's law, bodies always fall down and never up.

A rough and loose track leaves excitement behind and ascends the fellside above the Rock to the summit of the mountain. On this final stage it is well to look back and downwards to the top of High Man and its coveted cairn, which from this viewpoint assumes the shape of a dome with a fearful abyss on either side.

The High Level Route is not only the royal road to Pillar Rock but to Pillar mountain also.

High Man from the fellside

Summit cairn

THE SUMMIT: 2927 FT

All the interest of Pillar is centred on the Ennerdale side, the summit being a flat and stony expanse lacking natural features and depending on man's creations to relieve the monotony of the scene. A cairn, an Ordnance column and two wind shelters testify to the esteem in which Pillar is regarded by fellwalkers and the makers of maps. A broken wire fence of which only the posts remain, completes the immediate attractions. There is no awareness of imminent declivities all around, these being revealed only by a perambulation of the top. The distant view across the rather dull summit is magnificent in all directions. Great Gable and the entire Scafell range are seen to perfection, the northern fells and the Helvellyn group fill the horizon in great detail, and over the gulf of Windgap Cove an arresting skyline is formed by Scoat Fell, Steeple and the heights beyond as they decline to Ennerdale Water and the sea.

From the north windshelter, there is a sensational view down into Ennerdale with the High Man of Pillar Rock thrusting out of the steep fellside directly below.

The north-eastern fells from Pillar

Summit wall on Scoat Fell

THE MOSEDALE HORSESHOE

The ascent of Pillar from Wasdale Head can conveniently be extended into a classic expedition, with little further effort, by making a high-level circuit of the heights enclosing Mosedale: this is a horseshoe walk notable not for scenic beauty but for the extreme wildness of the terrain.

The summit of Pillar is left by a short path descending sharply to Wind Gap and the facing slope climbed to the flat top of Black Crag. A deviation to the rim of the cliff discloses a scene of profound desolation and across the wild recess of Mirk Cove Steeple is seen springing out of the stony debris of Windgap Cove: a primeval landscape where silence and solitude are absolute.

SCOAT FELL

Scoat Fell is directly ahead and its long sprawling top is reached along a rising path joined by a wall. The only distinction here is the absence of a summit cairn: Scoat Fell (2760 ft) is the one fell in Lakeland so deprived, the reason being that the highest inches are occupied by the wall, a substantial structure. However, not to be thwarted, enthusiasts for summit cairns have erected a pile of stones on its top.

Away from its interesting summit Scoat Fell has two features of note: one is the vast hollow of Mirklin Cove defended by a line of cliffs on the Ennerdale side, and the other is Scoat Tarn on the Wasdale flank.

But its main claim to fame is its close proximity to Steeple.

Red Pike and Scafell from Scoat Fell

STEEPLE

Steeple, owing allegiance only to Ennerdale, is strictly not within the itinerary of the Mosedale Horseshoe, but its delightful peaked summit is too good to miss. A short path from Scoat Fell goes down to a narrow col between Mirklin Cove and Mirk Cove and then rises to the neat top at 2681 ft: a diversion of a few minutes, although few who arrive there depart in a hurry. It is a thrilling place to linger, a lofty perch high above a petrified desert of stone where a commoner can sit like a monarch on a throne and survey a silent kingdom without life or movement, an awesome scene gripped by a deathly stillness. Within a stride, the ground collapses in crags in a tremendous plunge into the depths of Windgap Cove far below, and Mirk Cove alongside appears as a shattered crater: turning round, the cliffs of Mirklin Cove make an impressive façade to Scoat Fell.

It is a privilege to stand on the top of Steeple.

Summit of Steeple

RED PIKE

The return to Wasdale Head starts with an easy descent from Scoat Fell to a depression beyond which rises Red Pike, a mountain with two very different faces; that overlooking Mosedale is a fearful tumble of crags, the other is a gradual decline of sheep pasture to Nether Beck with a midway halt to contain the shy waters of Low Tarn.

The summit at 2707 ft has two large cairns widely spaced and near the further and lower one is a feature which was known to Victorian visitors and was named on the Ordnance maps at that time as The Chair. This is a natural arrangement of rocks to form a seat with arm and back rests; it is still there and still comfortable but today forgotten and usually passed unnoticed.

The walk continues easily down a ridge and arrives at a col below Yewbarrow. This is the infamous Dore Head and from it a scree-run descends into Mosedale; it was once a quick and pleasant way down but over the years it has been made slippery and dangerous by overuse and has been widened to the dimensions of a road by boots that have scraped away the verges in a search for firmer footing. Care is needed in descent.

A path is joined at the foot of the Dore Head screes and this leads through fields alongside Mosedale Beck where Ritson's Force is hidden amongst trees; and so back to Wasdale Head to complete a memorable day's adventure.

Wasdale Head

173

Scafell

3162 ft

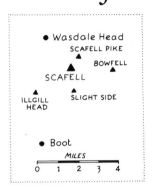

THE HIGHEST GROUND IN England is formed by the huge upthrust of the Scafell range south of Sty Head. The early settlers in Wasdale named the whole mass Scaw Fell, and later when it became necessary for the farmers and shepherds to identify the individual peaks in the group by name, the one that most dominated the valley with an awesome and superior presence retained exclusively the name of Scaw Fell. In due course, the Ordnance Survey amended the spelling to Sca Fell, two words, which common usage has telescoped into one, Scafell. This is the parent mountain in the family, and the greatest, measuring its authority not by altitude above sea level but by a magnificent natural feature that provides the grandest sight in Lakeland.

This feature, overwhelming in immensity, intimidating in appearance, is Scafell Crag, a tremendous wall of rock with vertical pitches split by cavernous gullies into towers and pinnacles. Here began the history of rock-climbing in the district a century ago when, against the advice of mine host at the inn at Wasdale Head ('nobbut a fleeing thing could get up theer'), the pioneers of the sport, brave men all, ventured to explore and test any structural weaknesses in the massive wall in a search for routes of ascent. Equipped only with ropes, they succeeded in making the impossible possible and in the course of a few years established a variety of climbs. Those were the great days of rock-climbing and the recorded exploits of Owen Glynne Jones and the Abraham brothers and their friends, illustrated by startling photographs, aroused an interest in the sport that has accelerated with the passing years.

Scafell Crag is palpably no place for a mere pedestrian who must be content to survey it from the safety of the green hollow below. The most memorable fellwalking experience of all is to witness the miracle of a new day from a summertime overnight bivouac here as the jet black silhouette of the crag imperceptibly changes to grey in the light of dawn, and then, in a wonderful moment, the upper rocks become diffused in a rosy glow as they are touched by the first rays of the sun. Very gradually the line of sunlight creeps down the face of the crag, dispersing the last ghosts of night, until the whole wrinkled face is revealed in detail: a play enacted in perfect stillness.

Opposite *Scafell from Lingmell*

Scafell and Mickledore from Wasdale

The chasm between Scafell Crag and the neighbouring Scafell Pike is crossed by a slender ridge carrying a path from one to the other. This is Mickledore, a place of spectacular grandeur where the mighty power of nature is manifest in the towering cliffs that leap into the sky on both sides. Here a walker is granted a free pass into the home of the gods and in the immensity of the surroundings made to feel insignificant, stripped of pride and arrogance, and reduced to abject humility. Here he is made to realise what a fleeting thing his life is as he surveys a scene that has not changed since the world began.

Above the Mickledore ridge, Scafell Crag loses its severity and the rocks become more broken on an easier strip of rising ground cut away along its edge by the cavernous rift of Mickledore Chimney. Immediately beyond the Chimney is another line of cliffs, the East Buttress. Of lesser height than the main crag, the East Buttress is even more hostile and forbidding; vertical and overhanging walls of rock give an appearance of total inaccessibility emphasised by dark shadow for most of the daylight hours. Yet this too has succumbed to the efforts of later generations of climbers aided by more modern equipment, and is now criss-crossed by a network of severe routes.

Above *Mickledore*   Below *East Buttress*

On the approach to Mickledore from Scafell Pike, the narrow strip of easy ground rising beyond the ridge is seen as a distinct breach between Scafell Crag and the East Buttress and appears to offer a direct way to the top of Scafell. This is a cruel delusion. Access to this promising ladder is barred by tiers of low rocks only a few feet high but sheer and difficult to climb. This is the infamous Broad Stand and is the most frustrating place in Lakeland for walkers who steer clear of rocks.

A crack, appropriately known as Fat Man's Agony, can be squeezed through from the Mickledore screes to a small sloping platform below a blank wall of rock bereft of hand- and foot-holds and eight feet high. Scratches on the left edge indicate the way to tackle this obstacle, but with the yawning gulf of Mickledore Chimney waiting to receive falling bodies directly below and a similar wall and broken rocks above, further progress has an unacceptable element of risk. Times without number I have stood on the platform with iron resolve melting, and palsied legs demanding retreat. It is galling to see rock-climbers romping up and down Broad Stand but for wise walkers it is definitely out of bounds.

Scafell is a mountain of massive bulk, the last high ground before the turbulent landscape of the fells settles down into the rural loveliness of Eskdale and the coastal fringe. The northern edge collapses in fearful precipices above the chasm of Mickledore and all the other slopes are steep; the eastern flank is particularly rough and craggy in marked contrast to the south and west sides where the ground cover is featureless grass. The summit is the culminating point of a long south ridge ending abruptly in the rocky top of Slight Side and rooted in the colourful foothills of Eskdale, a fascinating area with two hidden gems, Low Tarn and Stony Tarn, to delight explorers. The main watercourse is the River Esk, to which How Beck and Catcove Beck make handsome contributions, and the large sheet of water in the west, Burnmoor Tarn, is fed by Hardrigg Gill.

ASCENTS

There are several excellent ascents to the summit – Scafell is both monster and friend yet undeniably a king amongst mountains.

FROM ESKDALE

All routes from Eskdale are long, requiring a full day for completion and return.

The most direct way leaves the valley road opposite Wha House Farm, a terrace path rising gradually and pleasantly to come alongside Catcove Beck and its tributaries on a marshy plateau. Here, now without the help of a path, a beeline must be made to the top of Slight Side directly in front: this is a tiring treadmill up a steep slope that never relents until the delightful rocky top of Slight Side is reached, an occasion for a deserved halt. The summit ridge is now clearly in view ahead and is followed along the eastern edge to the highest point and its welcome cairn.

Right *Summit cairn, Scafell*
Opposite *Broad Stand*

Scafell from Great Moss

A longer but more beautiful route leaves from Brotherilkeld Farm and follows the Esk upriver to Great Moss at the foot of the mountain. The next objective is Cam Spout, a fine waterfall with a path climbing steeply alongside. Ahead, the gap of Mickledore is seen between the East Buttress and Scafell Pike and sets the direction for the next stage of the ascent but, before reaching the East Buttress, a straight gully coming down from an upper recess is the key to the easiest way to the summit. By scrambling up this gully, a tiny pool, little more than a puddle but given the name of Foxes Tarn, is reached; from here a simple scree slope above the East Buttress leads up to a skyline saddle with the summit then only five minutes away on the left.

From the top of Cam Spout an alternative route follows a rising ridge on the left, passing between the edge of Cam Spout Crag, and the recess of How Beck, and curves up to the summit ridge near the top.

Scafell and Cam Spout

180

FROM WASDALE HEAD VIA GREEN HOW

Much the simplest way of attaining the top of Scafell is provided by the western slope of Green How, a rising prairie of grass needing no direction except to keep the boots pointing upwards.

The old corpse road to Boot by Burnmoor Tarn gives a pleasant start but is departed from near its highest point to set foot on the fellside on the left and commence the long climb up the slopes of Green How. This is a tiring trudge innocent of interest although the tedium can be relieved somewhat by persevering along the edge overlooking Brown Tongue. When at last the grass gives way to scree, the journey becomes more exciting. The upper exit of Lord's Rake is reached and should be memorised for future identification. Now, with the guidance of a scree path and acutely aware of imminent danger on the left, the edge of the crags is followed upwards past the gaping gash of Red Gill to arrive at the easy saddle near the top of Deep Gill. Here the rock scenery is spectacular and sufficiently sensational to erase the toil of the ascent from the mind and make the effort seem well worthwhile. The summit cairn is now seen on the right and quickly reached.

Scafell from Green How

FROM WASDALE HEAD VIA BROWN TONGUE

The most thrilling walk in Lakeland reaches the top of Scafell by way of an ingenious passage that penetrates the rocks of Scafell Crag, taking advantage of a weakness in the structure of the mountain that admits to an exciting climb so steep that contours cannot be recorded, and higher than the tallest cathedral. Yet this entry into the secret portals of the crag is open to all active walkers, is quite safe, and will cause no suffering other than palpitations. Nature has here granted a rare privilege to pedestrians.

The path from Wasdale Head ascends Brown Tongue to arrive at the amphitheatre of Hollow Stones, passing below Black Crag, beyond which a wide and merciless slope of scree is seen coming down from Scafell Crag now fully revealed. This uncompromising downfall of stones was greatly augmented thirty years ago when a cloudburst hit the area during a severe electrical storm. A struggle up this unfriendly ladder of rock debris, preferably keeping alongside Black Crag, leads to the foot of Scafell Pinnacle in most impressive surroundings, the Pinnacle soaring above in a tower 500 feet in height. To the right at this point rises a steep narrow channel between rocks, and choked by stones and boulders. This is Lord's Rake, too obvious to be missed and identifiable exactly by a cross carved in the rock wall a few paces to the left; this marks the spot where the bodies of four climbers were found after a fall from the Pinnacle in 1903.

The next half hour will remain an evergreen memory for life.

Dramatic rock scenery

Lord's Rake is a surprise, an unexpected bounty of nature where all else is inaccessible and threatening. Here the cliffs of Scafell Crag are breached by a straight cutting rising diagonally across the downfall of crags to give entry into a wonderland created by a master architect. Lord's Rake is a ladder into realms of grandeur. But it is a ladder without rungs and, even for the most active, calls for strenuous effort.

Upward progress along the Rake is a desperate struggle against gravity and an unholy allegiance of wedged boulders and slippery stones. Soon after entering the narrow confines, the fearful rift of Deep Gill opens on the left, a place for cragsmen but causing ordinary mortals to shudder. Enclosed by rock walls that allow no escape, every foothold gained is a minor triumph. Clawing hands seeking security and leverage have scraped away the starry saxifrage that once decorated the damp crevices of the rocks, there is no worn path and every man must fend for himself. The top of this section of the Rake is a small col, reached after an eternity of arduous effort; this is succeeded by a second col after which a long descent crosses the scree debouching from Red Gill and finally rises to an exit on the open fellside. Thus ends Lord's Rake, a passage to remember.

But branching from the Rake just below the first col is an even more thrilling alternative: the West Wall Traverse.

Deep Gill Buttress

The West Wall Traverse is the ultimate and greatest privilege granted to fellwalkers in Lakeland, a safe incursion to the heart of Scafell Crag, an open invitation to witness at close range a display of rock sculptures of awesome proportions carved by a supreme creator, a silent and solemn assembly where man feels an intruder, a speck of life amongst giants of a dead past.

A few yards below the first col in Lord's Rake, the confining left wall relents, giving place to a low bank scoured to erosion by generations of boots and leading up to an easy terrace rising in a gentle incline and doubling back to enter Deep Gill above its lower difficulties. This terrace is a remarkable benefaction of nature, beset by perils on both sides yet totally free from hazards. The rock scenery is awe-inspiring: on the right the huge Deep Gill Buttress soars vertically upwards, on the left Lord's Rake is now a fearful chasm, and directly ahead is the upper part of Scafell Pinnacle, leaping in a single bound to a slender top. Deep Gill, at the point of entry, is seen as a steep and stony gully pointing the way between stupendous cliffs to the top of the mountain and can be followed up to its exit without trouble. The exit was once defended by an overhanging cornice of grass and earth but this obstacle has long since been pulled away to give access to easy ground. The summit cairn is in sight and is reached by a simple stroll in marked contrast to the trials of the last half-mile to end a wonderful adventure.

THE SUMMIT: 3162 FT

After the excitement of the ascent the summit is a rather disappointing anti-climax, tame and uninteresting; it inspires no emotion other than a feeling of achievement. If there is time for relaxation it is better spent at the top of Deep Gill admiring the magnificent rock formations to be seen there. Deep Gill Buttress towers on the left and Scafell Pinnacle on the right, the latter springing out of the depths to a delicate top isolated by a gap. Between the two, Great Gable is set in a rocky frame.

Descents from Scafell, whether bound for Eskdale or Wasdale, are most easily made by the western slope, passing over Green How to join the Burnmoor track. In mist or bad weather, no other way off the mountain should be considered.

As befits the second highest mountain in the country, the distant panorama is extensive and interrupted only by the greater bulk of Scafell Pike nearby, hiding Helvellyn: all the other major heights in the district, however, are clearly in view. Unseen is the mountain's finest feature, Scafell Crag, which drops out of sight completely and is unsuspected, only the fretted rim being visible. It is in the southern arc that the prospect excels: low foothills, lovely valleys and the sands of the Duddon and Esk estuaries leading the eye to a vast expanse of sea with the Isle of Man prominent, and on clear days everything can be seen in marvellous detail. Correspondents have claimed sightings of the mountains of North Wales and Ireland on days of exceptional visibility. Wastwater and several tarns complete a beautiful picture.

Rock scenery at the top of Deep Gill

Above *Pulpit Rock and Great Gable*   Below *Pikes Crag*

Scafell Pike

3210 ft

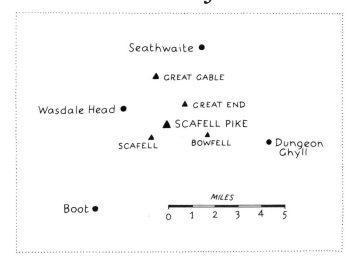

IT IS REMARKABLE THAT the highest mountain in England should suffer a confusion of names. Scafell Pike was obviously given the family name of the parent mountain, Scafell, the original spelling of both being Scawfell. The Ordnance Survey recognised three separate tops, including the then nameless peaks now known as Broad Crag and Ill Crag as adjuncts of the highest pike, identifying them on their maps as The Pikes of Scawfell, later amending this to Scafell Pikes. Finally in the 1980s, they dropped the 's'. Broad Crag and Ill Crag are now commonly regarded as separate entities from Scafell Pike.

Scafell Pike is massive, shapeless and without even a touch of elegance. It has outgrown the head of the family but inherited none of its grandeur, the tremendous facade of Scafell Crag facing the Pike wearing a perpetual frown of displeasure and disappointment. The best the Pike can do to appease the old man and emulate his greatness is seen in Pikes Crag opposite, impressive in itself but untidy and a poor imitation. Admiration and attention are focussed on Scafell Crag and, in such company, Pikes Crag is dismissed at a glance.

But superior altitude counts for much and the Pike is the magnet that attracts all active visitors to the district, giving them a sense of achievement: there is a unique satisfaction in standing on the very highest point in the country, an event usually commemorated by a personal celebration. Indeed, celebrations of all sorts from birthday parties and bonfire parties to reunions and memorial services have been held here. This is a very special place, and there is no other like it.

Scafell Pike is the supreme objective, the ultimate.

Opposite Scafell Pike from Great Moss

Scafell Pike is not an isolated mountain, sturdy support being given by adjacent heights that enjoy equal prominence in the landscape: indeed, in distant views it would be difficult to identify the Pike with certainty had it not the advantage of a slight overtopping of its fellows. On one side only is there an uninterrupted fall to valley level, eastwards into upper Eskdale; elsewhere substantial buttresses, each a mountain in its own right, limit its domain. In the south there is a connection with Scafell at Mickledore; westwards Lingmell intervenes to cut off the descent into Wasdale, and in the north Broad Crag and Ill Crag crowd alongside to form the trinity of peaks. Despite its height, the roots of Scafell Pike are stunted by close neighbours.

Scafell Pike is the culminating point on a lofty range which, with four separate summits exceeding 3,000 feet in height, is the most formidable mountain barrier in the Lake District and the roughest, much of it being a desert of stones. The range terminates abruptly at both extremities: Slight Side on Scafell overlooks Eskdale in the south and the well-named Great End falls away in cliffs facing Borrowdale in the north.

The northern part of the range from Broad Crag to Great End was part of a comprehensive purchase of land over 1,500 feet in height in the vicinity by the Fell and Rock Climbing Club in 1923 as a War Memorial to honour their members who fell in the First World War. This purchase included twelve mountain tops around Great Gable.

Scafell Pike was a later gift to the nation.

Looking to Esk Hause

Visitors on the popular approaches to Scafell Pike from Borrowdale or Great Langdale return with an impression of treading upon endless stones in a dull trudge, redeemed by excellent distant views but lacking features of immediate interest. They see nothing of the mountain's more dramatic aspects which are hidden and unsuspected from the tourist paths. On the route from Wasdale Head, too, there is little out of the ordinary apart from a glimpse of Pulpit Rock on Pikes Crag, a fine pillar with climbs for experts; and a classic view from its rocky top of Scafell Crag in wonderful detail and correct proportions. The Pike's best secrets are reserved for explorers on its east side where, low down, is the fine cliff of Dow Crag, also known as Esk Buttress, and the confines of Little Narrowcove. When these are seen, Scafell Pike will be regarded with more respect.

Pikes Crag   Above *Pulpit Rock*

Scafell Pike divides the waters of Eskdale and Wasdale which have a common destination in the Irish Sea, and has no influence in the valleys of Borrowdale and Great Langdale. It is, therefore, rather surprisingly, only a minor watershed. Nevertheless all the streams born on the mountain soon develop differences of character and temperament in their infancy. The River Esk drains the eastern side, augmented by the torrent descending Little Narrowcove and the waterfall of Cam Spout as it flows on its lovely journey to the sea. On the west flank is the frightful canyon of Piers Gill, the biggest rift in the Lakeland landscape which also has a waterfall, and the storm-ravaged Lingmell Gill; both enter the head of Wastwater. Tarns are absent, the only standing water being a pool on the Mickledore side which hardly deserves the name of Broadcrag Tarn.

ASCENTS

A variety of routes of ascent, all served by paths, is available leaving the valleys of Borrowdale, Great Langdale, Wasdale and Eskdale and all providing exhilarating walks in grand surroundings, all that is except the route from Wasdale Head which is shorter and steeper than the others.

If based in Borrowdale, there is a choice of two routes with the decided advantage of a return by the alternative; from Great Langdale, the route of ascent must be reversed for the return; from Wasdale a diversion is recommended when returning, and from Eskdale there are possibilities of variation but none to compare with the attractiveness of the usual approach.

Sprinkling Tarn and Great End

Esk Hause from Great Gable

FROM BORROWDALE VIA ESK HAUSE

The starting point is Seathwaite where a wide path trodden to dust goes upriver to Stockley Bridge, picturesque but a too popular picnic spot. Go across the bridge and, ignoring the more frequented path climbing the fellside to Sty Head, follow the stream up into the ravine of Grains Gill; the path emerges after a steep climb on the main pedestrian path between Great Langdale and Wasdale. At this point the delectable Sprinkling Tarn is nearby on the right, but this is a temptress whose invitations to linger must be repulsed, time being pressing. At this moment, too, Great End comes fully into sight.

A track now makes a beeline for Esk Hause with a view down into the upper reaches of Eskdale; it then climbs to the right to join the main ridge behind Great End. Progress becomes easier between widening contours but the hard work is not yet over since you need to watch your step as you cross a field of boulders before the stony path arrives at a dip in the ridge. Here, if you are ahead of schedule, the summit of Ill Crag may be reached by a diversion, and later Broad Crag also as the path slants upwards alongside. Finally, from a further depression, the footmarks of countless pilgrims point the way to the top of Scafell Pike.

FROM BORROWDALE VIA STY HEAD AND THE CORRIDOR ROUTE

Today's fellwalkers have good reason to be grateful to others who have gone before: to the earlier dalesfolk who engineered easy paths to some of the mountain summits for the passage of their Victorian guests, and especially to the pioneer rock-climbers who devised exciting short cuts to the crags, such as the High Level Route on Pillar, the Climbers' Traverse on Bowfell, the West Wall Traverse on Scafell and the Corridor Route to Pikes Crag and Scafell Crag, all of which have been adopted and enjoyed by walkers.

The Corridor Route, originally called the Guides' Route, is equally available for the ascent of Scafell Pike from Borrowdale. Starting from Seathwaite the busy path to Sty Head is taken from Stockley Bridge, and from there the line of the route is defined by an easy shelf crossing the rough western slopes of the range at mid-height. A slight descent is made to the outflow from the wild ravine of Skew Gill and after a rise the headwaters of Greta Gill, which has a magnificent unseen waterfall below the path, are crossed to skirt the top of the Piers Gill chasm.

The route then climbs gently to the Lingmell col and the summit of the Pike, guided by a multitude of cairns. A path also leaves the Corridor and aims for the Broad Crag col to give an alternative finish. The Corridor is an excellent return route if the ascent has been made by way of Esk Hause.

View taken from above the Corridor Route

Upper Eskdale and the Scafells, from Esk Hause

FROM GREAT LANGDALE

The ascent of Scafell Pike from Dungeon Ghyll in Great Langdale is often undertaken but suffers from two disadvantages: first, that the route must be reversed when returning, there being no alternative and, secondly, that the cascade of stones choking Rossett Gill must be trodden twice, both up and down. Otherwise this is a fine walk.

The route starts with a level two miles to the head of Mickleden, where those discerning walkers who have previously discovered the old pony route will prefer to use its easy inclines to get to the top of Rossett Pass but others less informed must resign themselves to a strenuous struggle against two enemies, gravity and stones, to arrive at the same place. Normal walking is now resumed with a gentle descent to the outflow of Angle Tarn, followed by a steady rise to the walled wind shelter at the highest point of the path. This is a popular halt. Here the main path, which now goes down to Sty Head and Wasdale, is left in favour of another leading up the fellside to Esk Hause and the graphic picture disclosed there of the upper reaches of Eskdale flanked by the massive Scafell range.

At Esk Hause the path is joined by another coming up from Borrowdale and climbs to reach the main ridge at a depression below the south slope of Great End which has loomed large in the landscape since leaving the wind shelter. At this point, walkers who are already tiring and are acutely aware that Scafell Pike is still far distant and that every step is taking them further from Great Langdale only to be retraced later, can change their plans and, without dishonour, climb to the summit of Great End instead. Let them be consoled by my assurance that it is a worthier objective than the Pike and has an exciting promenade along the edge of cliffs plus a superb view better than any obtained from the Pike. Others, more determined, will urge their boots forward along the path to Scafell Pike and achieve what they set out to do.

Scafell from Brown Tongue

FROM WASDALE

This route has the single merit of shortness but lacks sweetness, every step being relentlessly uphill in harsh surroundings, but to its credit walkers get an impressive view of the mighty Scafell Crag on the way.

A footbridge over Lingmell Beck at Wasdale Head points the way to a path rising across the Lingmell fellside where, upon turning a corner, the grim Scafell skyline bursts into view. The path fords Lingmell Gill, still not fully recovered from its battering during a severe storm half a century ago, and mounts the tedious slope of Brown Tongue. Interest quickens as the path arrives at the verges of an amphitheatre littered by boulders. This is Hollow Stones, deep-set below the cliffs of Pikes Crag on the left and the more imposing Scafell Crag on the right: a brutal scene, rather frightening on a first visit with a threat of disaster more apparent than real. The path escapes from this inferno of rocks by turning left below Pikes Crag to the safety of the Lingmell col from which a well-blazed track, marked by many unnecessary cairns spirals upwards without incident to the top of Scafell Pike.

If returning to Wasdale an alternative way of return to Brown Tongue is available and strongly recommended to all except the most timid of pedestrians by going down to and crossing the Mickledore ridge and descending therefrom into Hollow Stones immediately below the awesome precipice of Scafell Crag. In such a majestic presence man is cut down to size and quite unimportant in the general scheme of things. It is an experience that does him a power of good, or should.

FROM ESKDALE

The ascent from Eskdale is the most attractive of all, having a beautiful river for company most of the way, and furthermore is the only route that reveals Scafell Pike in full stature directly ahead as it is approached.

From Brotherilkeld Farm, a good path goes upriver alongside the Esk which abounds in inviting bathing pools that should be saved for the return journey. The quaint Lingcove Bridge is crossed to a path, still following the Esk now deep on the left and displaying waterfalls. The Pike comes into full view ahead, a fine object that spurs the footsteps towards it. At Great Moss the river is bade farewell and a steep climb made by the side of Cam Spout. Mickledore is ahead and is reached up a rough slope ending in scree, passing below the East Buttress of Scafell. The wonderful rock scenery of Mickledore stops all walkers in their tracks, and the stony path from there to the summit of the Pike is a tame anti-climax.

A more adventurous route, unfrequented and little known, persists upriver from Great Moss until past Dow Crag and then turns up the watercourse beyond and enters the pathless Little Narrowcove, a craggy ravine with an exit at the top which gives access to Broadcrag col and the tourist path from Esk Hause.

Scafell Pike from near Lingcove Bridge

The view from the summit shelter

THE SUMMIT: 3210 FT

The summit of Scafell Pike is also the summit of England, a distinction recognised in the proud days of the Empire by the erection on the highest point of a raised platform surmounted by steps and ringed by a substantial wall. This once handsome edifice is no longer in pristine condition, having been kicked out of shape by daily processions of visitors with no thought of the glories of Empire or respect for its monuments; from time to time efforts have been made to restore it. Set in the outer north wall is a tablet commemorating the gift of the summit to the nation, and nearby is an obsolete triangulation column of the Ordnance Survey, a reminder of the days when mapmakers travelled on foot and not in aeroplanes.

The top of Scafell Pike is a barren desolation of stones of all shapes and sizes, difficult to negotiate, uncomfortable to walk upon and worn to a comparative smoothness only where paths have been trodden. There is no beauty here and only one rare patch of vegetation where exhausted bodies can recline. As befits its unique status, the top is rugged, sturdy and strong – just as it should be.

Inevitably, the summit is often crowded and noisy, not at all a place for rest and meditation, and visitors seeking quietness and privacy will find these blessings by a short stroll to the unfrequented south summit overlooking Eskdale, a kinder place, free from litter, where the silence of the mountains can be enjoyed in peace.

It is to be expected that the summit of Scafell Pike would have the most far-reaching panorama in the country, and so it proves. All the major heights in Lakeland are in display in a view crowded with detail and extending across the Irish Sea to the Isle of Man and, on rare occasions, to the mountains of Snowdonia in North Wales, the Mountains of Mourne in Ireland and the Galloway Hills in Scotland. With many coastal features also in view, the identification of everything in sight is a task requiring more time than can normally be allotted to it. Most visitors are content to renew visual acquaintance with their Lakeland favourites from this superior elevation. The panorama is essentially of mountains; valleys and lakes are much less in evidence. It must be added that a complete all-round sighting is a bonus not often granted since the Pike is an avid collector of shrouds of mist and low clouds.

Pillar and Great Gable   Below *Slopes of Great Gable and Sty Head*

A description of Scafell Pike would be incomplete and inadequate without reference to the neighbouring heights that so closely support its massive frame, sturdy satellites that pay homage to the greatest of all.

BROAD CRAG

Most intimately attached is Broad Crag, 3054 ft. It is separated only by a narrow gap, the Broadcrag col, which carries the tourist path from Esk Hause and has recently acquired added significance by receiving a new path coming up from the Corridor Route.

Across the gap is the territory of Broad Crag which, despite topping 3000 feet, is not commonly regarded as a separate fell, its summit being rarely visited although the path passes within a hundred yards and is little lower in elevation. The reason for this strange neglect is not clear from a study of the map but palpably obvious at the site: away from the trodden path, Broad Crag is a virgin jungle of boulders, piled one on top of another and settled at all angles, with a remarkable propensity for breaking legs – a desert of cruel rocks, hostile and defiant. A small cairn on the highest boulders indicate that some brave soul once scrambled to the top, but very few turn aside to inspect it. Of the thousands of pilgrims who pass along the path every year, it is doubtful whether one even leaves the safety of the path to struggle in search of the cairn. Broad Crag is an outcast, totally unloved except by foxes.

The name derives from a line of cliffs above the Corridor Route, the east slope disappears in a cascade of stones into the depths of Little Narrowcove, and the whole is arid without running or standing water.

I am sure readers will agree that I should not inflict on Derry's brittle limbs the risk of taking a picture of the summit cairn.

Broad Crag

Ill Crag

ILL CRAG

Ill Crag is the third of the Scafell trinity and not generally recognised as a separate entity although, at 3040 ft, it tops the magical 3000 ft.

Ill Crag shares a common kinship with Broad Crag and both bear signs of a rough and undisciplined upbringing, but they are not twins in appearance or characteristics. Ill Crag is in fact the more unruly of the two.

The summit of Ill Crag is reached without difficulty by a short detour from the path to the Pike from Esk Hause but this patch of easy ground belies the true nature of the fell which, beyond the small peaked top, falls away in a chaotic tumble of crags into Upper Eskdale and Little Narrowcove; indeed the eastern aspect gives an impression of ferocious bad temper and is so repelling and defiant, so lacking in invitation, that it is best left well alone.

Ill Crag, however, has one redeeming feature: it is the only one of the three summits with any semblance of a graceful outline, rising as a shapely pyramid when seen from the east.

Ill Crag is also a counterfeit: aspirants for Scafell Pike arriving at Esk Hause on a first visit wrongly assume that Ill Crag, which is in full view from this point, is their objective; the Pike is hidden beyond and is a considerable march further. This is the only occasion when Ill Crag seems to have a grin on its rugged face.

GREAT END

Great End terminates the Scafell range in the north and, at 2984ft, is the only one of the five distinct summits denied a 3000-foot contour. It is not however at all the least worthy and in some respects is superior to the others.

Great End thrusts boldly into space like a mighty headland, its height emphasised by a sudden collapse into cliffs, giving a commanding prominence when seen from other parts of the district; it is excellent as a viewing station.

The summit, easily reached from the path above Esk Hause, has two handsome cairns, widely spaced, and the walk between them along the edge of the cliffs, punctuated by thrilling peeps down the three gullies that split the cliffs from top to bottom, is a pleasant stroll enhanced by an absence of crowds and litter. From the west cairn, Great Gable is revealed in detail above the hollow of Sty Head but the gem of the view, a classic, is the full length of Borrowdale to Skiddaw. Scafell Pike has nothing to show more fair. Great End is a great end to the Scafell range.

Above *A summit cairn*   Below *View from Great End*

Wastwater from Lingmell

LINGMELL

Lingmell at 2649 ft is a staunch supporter of the Scafells, serving as a western buttress yet standing aside deferentially as though aware that height is a measure of greatness and that its modest altitude keeps it out of the big-time league. But, like Great End, it has attributes the 3000-footers lack, notably an exciting situation, easier conditions underfoot and a view ranking amongst the finest in the district.

Formerly a tall and elegant cairn crowned the summit but this was wrecked by vandals who find apparent pleasure in destroying the creations of others: volunteers replaced it.

Two views are of outstanding merit, one the superb full-height view of Great Gable from the top of Lingmell Crag, the other a comprehensive picture of Mosedale from the curving ridge going down to Lingmell Gill which, incidentally, offers an excellent return route to Wasdale from the Pike.

Skiddaw

3053 ft

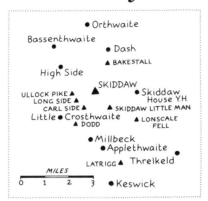

GEOLOGISTS TELL US THAT Skiddaw is the oldest mountain in Lakeland and that once upon a time it was covered by the sea, the evidence being seen in its rocks which are mainly marine deposits of soft shale or slate that split readily into thin wafers, decay when exposed to the atmosphere and have no commercial value.

One does not have to be a geologist to appreciate that Skiddaw is very different from the rugged volcanic mountains in the central part of the district: the slopes are smooth, sleek and grassy, there is an absence of crags of interest to rock-climbers and the stones covering the summit and exposed in eroded gullies are not at all like those that litter the Wasdale peaks. Skiddaw was formed long before the rest of Lakeland took shape and overlooked a vast glacier system, a world of ice. Some volcanic rocks are scattered along the lower southern slopes, these having been identified as originating in St. John's in the Vale and deposited when the glaciers retreated and scoured the fellsides in their passage to the frozen sea.

Skiddaw is the fourth highest peak in Lakeland and geographically the most important. Completely isolated by the Vale of Keswick and surrounded by lesser supporters which form a close-knit family group, it rises proudly in their midst like an old hen with a brood of chicks. The group dominates the northern landscape, springing steeply in a single bound from the valley pastures to a cluster of summits around the main peak, a noble assembly, graceful in outline and compelling admiration. Streams feed the rivers Derwent, Ellen and Caldew, all destined for the Solway Firth, draining a wide coastal plain. Because of the nature of the underlying rocks, Skiddaw has no mineral wealth and there are no quarries or mines. Agriculture on a small scale in the sheltered valleys is the only industry, mainly devoted to sheep farming, but this will be joined by another activity when the new conifer plantations above Bassenthwaite Lake come to maturity. Above these narrow limits of cultivation all the high ground of the group is a barren and untamed wilderness.

Opposite *Skiddaw from Surprise View*

Skiddaw from Keswick

Skiddaw is the hub, the focal point of the northern fells, a compact mass of high ground rising abruptly from low lying valleys on all sides, a lonely territory where nature has been left undisturbed: it is also the John Peel country of ballad and legend. Much of the area is known as Skiddaw Forest but it is a landscape of bare rolling fells and barren wastes without trees; everywhere is shrouded in silence. Skiddaw has long been a popular objective for visitors, but only recently since the central and southern parts of Lakeland have become more crowded have walkers begun to explore the northern fells and found solitude and peace there. Around the fringes are signs of man's exploitation for minerals but the interior is a vast sheep pasture in an environment as old as time.

Skiddaw is the proud and unchallenged overlord of a domain of quiet and sombre beauty, remote and unchanged in a world of change.

Skiddaw and Keswick go together, hand in hand in a bond of friendship. Through the centuries, the mountain has nurtured the town in its lap and provided many benefactions: it has supplied pure water, irrigated the fields and meadows, fed the sheep, offered a playground for recreation, given employment and assisted the local economy, sheltered the town from northerly gales, acted as a barometer of the weather, shared in celebrations and rejoicings, served as a warning beacon in times of troubles and, not least, contributed to the scenic beauties of the area by forming a permanent and colourful tapestry as a backcloth of great distinction.

Keswick folk for their part are brought up with an inborn affection for the giant on their doorstep. They are grateful for the many acts of benevolence and regard the mountain with a respect near to reverence. Life without Skiddaw is unthinkable.

ASCENTS

The time-honoured way to the top of Skiddaw, on a path trodden by thousands every year and first devised for the comfort of visitors on ponyback, climbs the southern slopes from Keswick. This is a safe route in any weather except deep snow, although free from obstacles and danger, it is rather tedious. Some early Victorians reported a sense of horror as they looked down from the upper heights, complaining of feeling faint but today's walkers are made of sterner stuff and infants and grandmothers are often seen in the summertime processions up the mountain.

Many other routes of ascent are available, but rarely used. A poll of visitors arriving at the summit would show that a walker ascending by a different route would be a very rare occurrence.

FROM KESWICK

The usual starting point is the terminus of Gale Road from Applethwaite where there is space for parking cars. Walkers not blessed with their own means of transport will probably reach the same spot by passing over the top or side of Latrigg as a preliminary, the pleasant lanes between there and Keswick now being cut into by the re-aligned A66.

The path leaves the road at a signpost and soon passes a monument, a memorial to three men of the Hawell family, shepherds of Lonscale; it bears the following inscription:

'Great Shepherd of Thy heavenly flock,
These men have left our hill
Their feet were on the living rock,
Oh guide and bless them still.'

Moving words; a good epitaph for fellwalkers. Further the original path has been varied by a newer and more direct one; either may be taken and both meet after a steady climb at the site of a former refreshment hut, a welcome halt in the old days, patronised by all who passed. Sadly it did not survive the last war. It was known as the Halfway House.

The path persists steeply up the fellside and upon reaching easier gradient veers to the left across an open grassland, bypassing Skiddaw Little Man and arrives amongst stones at a prominent cairn, fondly imagined to be the top of Skiddaw until, on arrival, the true summit, High Man, is seen to be half a mile further.

The Hawell monument

FROM MILLBECK

Two routes are available. One starts pleasantly enough along a good path to the weir on Mill Beck and continues alongside the descending stream, Slades Beck to and beyond its source, arriving at the Carlside col. Here a steep and excessively stony turn to the right leads up to the south top of Skiddaw with the summit an easy half mile further. This route is not suitable for walkers who like to proceed in a dignified manner: it becomes a ladder of stony debris, is closely confined by steep fellsides, is claustrophobic and has no views.

The other route, although mainly without a path, is much to be preferred. This takes immediately to the fellside of Doups and arrives at an area of striated rocks known as White Stones above the plantations of Dodd, thereafter continuing to the cairn on Carl Side and crossing the Carlside col to the final rise of Skiddaw.

White Stones, Carl Side

Carlside col

FROM RAVENSTONE

There is no doubt in my mind that by far the best approach to the top of Skiddaw is by way of its north-west ridge. This offers a fine expedition along a narrow crest in exciting surroundings and provides excellent views throughout, while a further consideration in its favour is solitude, a freedom from the constraining influence and distractions of others, since the route is not widely known and is usually unfrequented. And for collectors of summits here are three, all in line waiting to be ticked off in addition to Skiddaw.

The walk starts from the Ravenstone Hotel, five miles out of Keswick on the Carlisle road and this point can be reached by bus. A lane alongside the hotel grounds leads up by the edge of Dodd Wood to the open fell. Ullock Pike is ahead but too daunting for direct assault, and a wide sweep round to the left is made to reach its descending ridge, known as the Edge. What follows is sheer delight: with the Southerndale valley deep on the left, the Edge rises in minor undulations to the sharp peak of Ullock Pike, looking uncannily like a baby Matterhorn, a climb so pleasant that the top is reached almost with regret. This summit is delectable: a tiny perch amongst heather with a wonderful view over Bassenthwaite and over the coastal plain to the sea. The ridge goes on to the next summit, Long Side, on the brink of cliffs falling into Southerndale.

The next objective along the ridge is Carl Side but this summit may be bypassed by taking a direct line for the Carlside col now in sight where an insignificant pool rejoices in the name of Carlside Tarn but does not deserve either a name or a photograph. From the col there is a startling retrospective view of Long Side and Ullock Pike, their long fringe of crags now fully seen. Across the col, a steep and unpleasant scramble up a tilted desert of scree emerges at the south top of Skiddaw with the highest summit beyond.

Dash Valley   *Dead Crags*

FROM THE HIGH SIDE – ORTHWAITE ROAD

The two western valleys of Southerndale and Barkbethdale offer routes of ascent but both are unfrequented except by shepherds and sheep. Access to both valleys is from the farm of Barkbeth, reached by a narrow road branching off the country lane linking the hamlets of High Side and Orthwaite, and where it would be advisable to seek permission before proceeding further since there are no official rights of way. Both valleys carry streams converging at Barkbeth.

Southerndale, after a pleasant start, is the most impressive but least attractive of the two routes, being darkly shadowed by the steep fellsides of Ullock Pike and Long Side and ending with a scramble up to the Carlside col. In its lower reaches, there is a good path that dwindles to a thin track and finally fades to nothing.

Barkbethdale, running parallel to the north, is a brighter place and served by sledgates and drove roads but the final stiff pull up to the north col of Skiddaw has no such help and is arduous.

The two valleys are separated by a distinct ridge, named in sections as Little Knott, Great Knott, Buzzard Knott and Randell Crag, the latter having a group of surface rocks alien to the character of Skiddaw. This ridge offers an alternative ascent, pathless but more direct; the final scree slope, however, is an abomination.

Another route of greater merit, revealing two features of scenic interest – one the Skiddaw group's only waterfall and the other a petrified avalanche of rocks – also leaves the Orthwaite road and enters the Dash valley on the rough access road to Skiddaw House, formerly shepherds' cottages and now used as an hostel. Beyond the last farm, Dash Beck tumbles down the fellside in a series of spectacular falls known as Whitewater Dash: a short detour to this attractive display is rewarding. Opposite across the access road are Dead Crags, falling from the summit of Bakestall which is attained by climbing alongside the crags with a fence as guide, its services in this capacity continuing to the north col, the north top and the High Man of Skiddaw. This route too is tourist-free.

THE SUMMIT: 3053 FT

Skiddaw is not universally acclaimed as one of the great mountains of Lakeland. Its noble proportions are acknowledged but the smooth green slopes have sometimes led to it being described as not more than a grassy hill. Let those who belittle the status of this venerable old patriarch climb up to the highest cairn, for surely none will deny that the summit of Skiddaw is the summit of a true mountain, loftily overtopping all around, exposed to the elements, roughly paved with the debris of creation and demanding respect.

The summit takes the form of a long ridge exceeding 3000 feet in height throughout and it is stony everywhere. It has four minor undulations in a straight line on a north-south axis: the south top, the middle top, the main top (High Man) and the north top. An Ordnance column identifies the main top in misty conditions and there are crude wind shelters that give some protection against strong winds but none against rain. The sides of the ridge fall away sharply, inducing a feeling of being suspended in space far above the world below.

Make no mistake. Skiddaw is a mountain, a great mountain.

The summit ridge, looking south

View from Skiddaw looking south-west

An unsurpassed panorama greets the visitor to the summit of Skiddaw on a day of clear visibility, an all-round picture so magnificent and presented in such wonderful detail that his departure will be delayed for hours if he seeks to identify everything in sight. Most attention may be focussed in the southern arc where the heights of central Lakeland are arranged for inspection and form a turbulent skyline: eastwards are the nearby northern fells with the distant Pennines in the background, and to west and north uninterrupted views of the Cumbrian coast, the Irish Sea and the Isle of Man; across the Solway Firth can be seen the hills of Galloway, Criffell and the southern uplands of Scotland.

If I were asked by a stranger to the district to recommend a single climb that would give him a superb panorama I would send him up Skiddaw.

SKIDDAW LITTLE MAN

Skiddaw has an understudy, a fine upstanding fellow of the same age and definitely deferential to the old master. It guards the approach and scrutinises everybody who comes up from Keswick to pay their respects yet it has no hope of succeeding in popular esteem. This is Skiddaw Little Man which is usually bypassed on the way to the greater summit and considered to be of little consequence. This is rather unfair because the Little Man has independent features of interest and offers, to adventurous spirits only, an alternative route of ascent, direct, without a path or cairns to guide, and guaranteed free from human company.

This starts very pleasantly from Millbeck, following the good path upstream to the weir, where the Little Man is fully in view, and then tackles the steep slope descending from it, passing through three zones of vegetation: bracken, heather and grass. It arrives on the skyline at a small eminence I call Lesser Man, Little Man being a short stroll to the left. A rougher route, for super-adventurers only, continues upstream from the weir until Black Beck joins in. The route follows the stream up to its source and then climbs left to the south-west arête of Little Man which gives an exciting finish and scores a bull's-eye by arriving precisely at the summit cairn.

The summit of Little Man, at 2837 ft, is marked by a large pile of stones and overlooks the vast hollow of natural debris below the south top of Skiddaw, a no-man's land and a refuge for foxes.

In one respect the summit is supreme above all others for it commands the most beautiful and comprehensive view of the Lake District, as seen overleaf – a fitting conclusion to this book.

View from Skiddaw, looking east Below *Skiddaw from Little Man*
Overleaf *The Vale of Keswick and Derwentwater*

Index

Page numbers in **bold** refer to main entries. *Italic* numbers refer to the illustrations

Aaron Slack, 90, **92**, 95, 99, 101
Abraham brothers, vii, 163, 175
Adam-a-Cove, 43, 46
Addacomb Hole, 59
Allen Crags, 75, 76, 77
Ambleside, 70, 133
Angle Tarn, 27, 134, 193
Arthur's Pike, 141

Bad Step, 44, 46
Baddeley, 59
Bakestall, 208
Band, The, **22–3**, *22*, 27, 29, 42
Bannerdale, 17
Bannerdale Crags, 17
Barkbethdale, 208
Barrow Mine, 54
Bassenthwaite, 146, 203, 207
Beck Head, 90, **94**, *94*, 97, 101
Bessyboot, *76*, 78
Big Stack, 103, 104, 105
Birkhouse Moor, 117, **121**
Birks, 66
Black Crag, 171, 181
Black Sail Pass, 164
Black Sails, 39
Blackbeck Tarn, 103, 105, 106
Blea Water, 132, *132*, 136, 137, 138
Blea Water Crag, 132, 136, 138, *138*
Bleaberry Comb, 124, *124*, 127, 129
Bleaberry Tarn, 123, 124, 125, 127
Blease Fell, 4, **6**, 11, 12
Blease Gill, 4, **6**, *6*, 7
Blencathra, **1–19**, *1–19*, 27, 77, 138; ascents, 6–17; summit, 19
Blencathra Sanatorium, 6
Bonscale Pike, 141
Boo Tarn, 32, *34*
Borrowdale, 6, 12, 28, 51, 75, 76, *76*, 79, *79*, 90, 92, 96, 188, 189, 190–1, 192, 200
Boulder Valley, **34**
Bowfell, **21–9**, *21–9*, 41, 42, 45, 46, *46*, 77, 158, 192; ascents, 22–9; Eskdale flank, 29; summit, 28
Bowfell Buttress, 25, 27

Braithwaite, *vii*, 61, 82, 143, 144, 146
Brandreth, 93, 95, 103
Brim Fell, 37
Broad Crag, 187, 188, 191, 192, **198**, *198*, 199
Broad Stand, 179, *179*
Brotherilkeld, 29
Brown Tongue, **181**, 194
Browncove Crags, 113, *113*, 114
Brownrigg Well, 113, 118
Bull Crag, 78
Burnmoor Tarn, 179, 181
Bursting Stone Quarry, 32
Burtness Comb, 124, 126, *127*, 129
Buttermere, 52, 59, 61, 63, 81, 84, 86, 93, 96, 103–6, *107*, 123–9, *123*, *126–8*

Caldbeck Fells, *13*
Cam Spout, 180, *180*, 190, 195
Cambridge Crag, 24, *25*
Carl Side, 206, *206*, 207
Carlside col, 206, 207, *207*, 208
Caspel Gate, 136
Castle Crag, *75*
Castlenook, 52, 53, *54*, 54
Castlerigg Stone Circle, *2*, 4
Cat Rock, 100, *100*
Catbells, 54, 56, *56*
Catstycam, 116, **120**
Causey Pike, 59, 60, 62
Chair, The, 173
Chapel Crags, 124, 127, 129
Church Beck, 32, 33
Cinderdale Beck, 83, *83*, 84
Climbers' Traverse, The, **24–5**, *24*, 192
Cockley Beck, 43
Cockpit, The, 141
Cofa Pike, 66, 69, 72
Cold Pike, **48–9**, *48–9*
Coledale, 59, 60, *61*, 144, 146
Coledale Beck, 61
Coledale Hause, 59, *59*, 60, 61, 63, 81, **82**, 84, 86, 143, **144**, 145

Coleridge, S.T., 19, 117
Comb Gill, 75, 76, 78, 79
Comb Head, 75, 78, 79, *79*
Coniston Horseshoe, **37–9**
Coniston Old Man, **31–9**, *31–9*, 77, 96, 138; ascents, 32–4; Coniston Horseshoe, 37–9; Dow Crag, 36; summit, 35; Tilberthwaite Gill, 39
Coniston Water, 35
Coppermines Valley, *32*, **33**, 39
Corridor Route, **192**, *192*, 198
Crinkle Crags, 28, 29, **41–9**, *41–9*, 77; ascents, 42–3; Cold Pike, 48–9; summit, 46; traverse, 44–5
Crinkle Gill, 41, *41*, **42**
Cross Fell, 19
Crummock Water, 63, 81, 123, 125, 128, 129, *129*, 143, 146

Dale Head, **51–7**, *51–7*, 106; ascents, 52–4; Newlands Horseshoe, 56–7; Old Mines at Newlands, 54; summit, 55
Dalehead Copper Mine, 53, *53*, 54
Dalehead Tarn, 51, 52, 53, 56
Dash valley, 208, *208*
Dead Crags, 208, *208*
Deep Gill, 181, 182, 183, 184, *183–4*
Deepdale, *65*, 66, 68
Derwent, River, 17, 59, 75, *93*, 203
Derwentwater, 6, 12, 19, 56, *56*, 62, 76, 77, 146, *212*
Dixon Memorial, *116*, 117
Dodderwick Force, 136
Doddick Fell, **10**, 11
Doddick Gill, 4, 9, **10**, *10*
Dollywaggon Pike, 112, *112*, **120**
Dore Head, 173
Dove Crag (Fairfield), 70, 71, *71*, 72
Dove Crags (Grasmoor), 81, 82, **83**, 86
Dovedale, 71, *71*
Dovenest Crags, 79
Doves Nest Caves, 79
Dow Crag (Coniston), **36**, *36*
Dow Crag (Scafell Pike), 189, 195

Dubs Bottom, 105
Dubs Quarry, 105, 106
Duddon Valley, 34, 35, 36, 41, 43, 46, 48, 184
Dungeon Ghyll, 154, *154–5*, **155**, 156, 157, 193
Dunmail Raise, 112

Eagle Crag, 124, 129
East Buttress (Scafell), 176, *177*, 179, 180, 195
Easy Gully, **161**
Eden Valley, 17, 19
Edge, The, 207
Eel Crag, **59–63**, *59–63*, 81, 82, 146; ascents, 60–2; summit, 63
Eel Crags, 52, 56, *57*
Ennerdale, 94, 96, 103, 123–5, 127, 128, 164, 166, 170, 172
Ennerdale Water, 128, 164, 170
Esk, River, 28, 29, 179, 180, 184, 190, 195
Esk House, 76, *188*, **191**, *191*, 192, 193, *193*, 195, 198, 199, 200
Esk Pike, 27
Eskdale, 28, *28*, 29, 41, 42, 46, 96, 179, 184, 188, 190, 191, 193, *193*, 195, 196, 199
Esthwaite Water, 46

Fairfield, **65–73**, *65–73*; ascents, 66; Fairfield Horseshoe, 65, **70–3**; summit, 68–9
Far Tongue Gill, 53, 54
Fisher Gill, 111, 114
Flat Crags, 25, *25*
Force Crag, 59, 61
Foule Crag, 12
Froswick, 135, 139

Gable Crag, 53, *53*, 89, 92, 97, 101
Gable Girdle, **98–101**
Gamlin End, 126, 127, 128
Garburn Pass, 139
Gasgale, 143, 146
Gasgale Gill, 60, *60*, 63, 81, 82, 83, 84, 145
Gate Gill, 4, **8**, *8*, 9, *9*
Gategill Fell, 6, 7, *7*, 8
Gategill Fell Top, 6, 7, *7*, 8
Gatesgarth, 104, 105, 129
Gatherstone Beck, 164
Gavel Neese, **94**, 97
Gillercomb, 93
Gimmer Crag, 153, *153*, 156, 159
Gladstone's Finger, 42, *42*
Glaramara, **75–9**, *75–9*; ascents, 76; Rosthwaite Fell, 78–9; summit, 77

Glenamara Park, 66
Glenderamackin, River, 12, **16–17**, *17*
Glenderaterra Beck, 6, 12, *13*
Glenridding, 116
Glenridding Beck, 121
Glynne Jones, Owen, vii, 175
Goat's Hause, 36
Goats Water, 36, *36*
Goldscope Mine, 55, 57
Gough, Charles, 118
Grains Gill, 75, 76, 191
Grasmere, 66, 73, 112
Grasmoor, 59, 60, 77, **81–6**, *81–7*, 106, 146; ascents, 82–5; summit, 86
Grasmoor End, *84*, 85, 86
Great Carrs, 39
Great Cove, 44, 45
Great Dodd, 121
Great End, 75, 77, 188, *190*, 191, 193, **200**, *200*, 201
Great Gable, 28, 55, 77, *77*, **89–101**, *89–101*, 103, 106, 128, 138, 170, 184, *185*, 188, *191*, 197, 200, 201; ascents, 92–5; descents, 95; Gable Girdle, 98–101; Moses' Trod, 97; summit, 95–6
Great Hell Gate, 99–100, *99*
Great How Crags, 37
Great Knott, 42
Great Langdale, 21, 22, 26–9, 41, 42, 45, 46, 149, 150, 152, 155, 189–91, 193
Great Moss, 180, *180*, *187*, 195
Great Napes, 89, 98, 99–100
Great Rigg, 66, 68, 72–3
Green Crag, 105, *105*
Green Gable, 89, 92, **93**, *93*, 101, *101*
Green Hole, 29
Green How, *163*, **181**, *181*, 184, *194*
Greenburn Valley, 37
Greenhow End, 66, 69
Greta, River, 17, 111
Greta Gill, 192
Grey Crag, 124, 129
Grey Knotts, 93, 95
Grisedale Beck, 117
Grisedale Hause, 66, 68, **112**
Grisedale Pike, *vii*, *85*, 143, **144**, **146**
Grisedale Tarn, 109, **112**, 118, 120
Gunson Knott, 45

Hall's Fell, 8, **9**, *9*, 10, 11, 19
Hanging Haystacks, 78
Hanging Knotts, 27

Hard Tarn, 110, 120
Harrison Combe, 156
Harrison Stickle, 150–2, *152*, 154, 155, *156*, **156–8**, *158–9*, 159
Hart Crag, 66, 72
Harter Fell, 136, 138
Hawell monument, 205, *205*
Hawes End, 56
Haweswater, 136, 138, 140
Hay Stacks, **103–7**, *103–7*; ascents, 104–5; summit, 106
Hayeswater, *132*, 134
Hell Gate Pillar, 99
Hell Gill, 23
Helvellyn, vii, 14, 19, 77, 106, **109–21**, *109–21*, 128, 138, 146, 158, 164, 170, 184; ascents, 112–17; Hellvellyn Range, 120–1; monuments, 117–18; summit, 118
Helvellyn Gill, **113**, *113*, 114
Hevellyn Lower Man, 111, 114, 118, **120**
Heron Pike, 73
Heughscar Hill, 141
High Bakestones, *70*
High Borrans, 139
High Crag (Haystacks), 104, 106
High Crag (High Stile), 123, 124, **126**, *126*, 127, 128
High Level Traverse, **166**, *166*
High Man, *168*, 168, *169*
High Moss, 62
High Pike, *70*, 70–1
High Raise, 139, 140
High Scawdel, 51
High Spy, 52, 56, *57*
High Spying How, 117
High Stile, 77, **123–9**, *123–9*; ascents, 124–6; summit, 127–8; traverse of the ridge, 128–9
High Street, **131–41**, *131–41*; ascents, 134–6; High Street ridge, 138–41; Roman Road, 133; summit, 137–8
High Sweden Bridge, 70
Hinckler, Bert, 118
Hindscarth, 51, *51*, 52, 53, 57
Hobcarton Crag, 143, 144, 145, 146
Hollow Stones, 181, 194
Honister Fell, 129
Honister Pass, 51, 52, **93**, 95, 105
Hope Gill, **145**, *145*
Hopegill Head, **143–6**, *143–7*; ascents, 144–5; summit, 146

Ill Bell, 133, 135, 139
Ill Crag, 187, 188, 191, **199**, *199*
Innominate Tarn, 103, 105, *106*

Irish Sea, 77, 96, 190, 196, 210
Isle of Man, 35, 96, 184, 196, 210

Jack's Rake, **161**, *161*
Jenkinson, 1, 59, 155

Keldas, 121, *121*
Kentmere, 132, 134, 135, *135*, 137, 139, *139*
Keppel Cove Tarn, 111, 121
Kern Knotts, *98*, 99, *99*
Keswick, 204–5, *204*, 210
Keswick, Vale of, 146, 203, *212*
Kidsty Pike, *131*, 136, 139
Kirk Fell, 89, *90*, 101
Kirkstone Pass, 134
Knott, 134
Knott Halloo, 7
Knowe Crags, 6

Lad Hows, **83**, 86
Lad Stones, 39
Ladyside Pike, *143*, 145
Langdale Pikes, 21, 28, 77, **149–61**, *149–61*; Dungeon Ghyll, 155–7; Harrison Stickle, 156–8; Loft Crag, 153; Pavey Ark, 159–61; Pike o' Stickle, Stickle Gill *156*, 151; stone axe factory, 152; Thorn Crag, 154
Langstrath, 27, 28, 77, 79
Langstrath Beck, 75
Lanthwaite, 60, 82, 145
Lanthwaite Hill, *82*
Lanty's Tarn, 121
Latrigg, 205
Levers Hause, 37
Levers Water, **33**, *33*, 39
Levers Water Beck, 33, 34
Lincomb Tarn, *76*
Ling Comb, 124, 125, 129
Lingcove Beck, 41, 42, 43
Lingcove Bridge, 29, 195, *195*
Lingmell, *92*, *175*, 188, 192, 194, **201**, *201*
Lingmell Beck, 89, 90, 92, 194
Lingmell Gill, 190, 201
Links, The, *23*, *23*, 29, 45
Little Hell Gate, 94, 100–1
Little How Crags, 37
Little Langdale, 39
Little Narrowcove, 189, 190, 195, 198, 199
Little Stand, 43
Little Town, 52, 53, 54
Littledale, 57
Liza, River, 89, 90, 94, 97, 164
Loadpot Hill, 140–1
Loft Crag, 150, *151*, **153**, *153*
Long Side, 207, 208

Long Top, 44–5, *44*, 46, *48*
Looking Stead, 164, 166
Lord's Rake, 181–2, *183*
Loughrigg Fell, *73*
Low Hartsop, 132, 134
Low Pike, 70, *70*
Low Water, 34
Low Water Beck, 34
Loweswater, 146
Lowther House, 140, *140*

Maiden Moor, 56, *56*
Mardale, 134, 136, 138, 139
Mardale Green, 131, 132
Mardale Head, 136, *136*, 137
Martindale, 140
Mickleden, 22, *22*, 24, 27, 151, 193
Mickledoor, 42, 45, *45*, 46
Mickledore, 176, *176–7*, 179, 180, 188, 194, 195
Middle Tongue, 8
Millbeck, 206
Mill Beck, 206
Mill Gill, 156
Mirklin Cove, 171, 172
Moor Divock, 139, 141, *141*
Morecambe Bay, 35, 69, 118, 138
Mosedale, 43, 46, 164, 173, 201
Mosedale Beck, 41
Mosedale Horseshoe, 171–2
Moses' Trod, **97**, *97*
Mungrisdale, 17

Nab Scar, 68, 73
Napes Needle, 100, *100*
Narrow Edge, 9
Near Tongue Gill, 53
Nethermost Cove, 112, 117, 120
Nethermost Pike, 100, 112, *112*, 113, **120**
Newlands, 51, 52, 59
Newlands Beck, 53, 54
Newlands Horseshoe, **56–7**
Newlands Valley, 52–3, 54, 55, 62, 63

Ore Gap, **27**
Orthwaite, 208
Oxendale, 22, 23, 41, 42

Patterdale, 66, 116–17, 134, 139
Pavey Ark, 150, 153, 157, 158, **159–61**, *159*, *161*
Peel, John, 2, 12, 204
Pennines, 17, 19, 28, *114*, 133, 210
Penrith, 19, 138
Piers Gill, 190, 192
Pike How, *156*
Pike o'Blisco, 22

Pike o'Stickle, 22, 150, **151–2**, *151–3*
Pikes Crag, *185*, 187, 189, *189*, 192, 194
Pillar, 28, 77, *77*, 103, 106, 128, 138, **163–73**, *163–73*, 192, *197*; ascents, 164–9; Mosedale Horseshoe, 171–3; summit, 170
Pillar Rock, *166*, **168–9**
Prison, The, 37
Prison Band, 39
Pudding Stone, 34
Pulpit Rock, *185*, 189, *189*

Rainsborrow Crag, 135, 139
Raise, **121**
Raise Beck, 111, 112
Rampsgill Head, 139
Randell Crag, 208
Rannerdale Beck, 60, 81
Raven Crag, 93
Ravenstone, 207
Red Dell Beck, 33
Red Dell Head, *31*
Red Gill, **84**, *84*, 86
Red Pike (High Stile), 123, 124, **125**, *125*, 127, 129
Red Pike (Pillar), *172*, **173**
Red Tarn (Crinkle Crags), 42, 43, 44, 49
Red Tarn (Helvellyn), 110, *111*, **116**, 117, 118, 120, 121
Rest Gill, 41, 43, *43*
Rigg, 136
Rigg, Moses, 97
Rigg Beck, 62
Rigg Head, 56
Riggindale, 132, 134, 136, 139
Ritson's Force, 173
Robinson, Harold, 14
Robinson, John Wilson, 166
Robinson's Cairn, *166*
Rock of Names, **117**
Roman Road, 131, 133, 137
Rossett Gill, 24, **26–7**, 193
Rosthwaite Cam, *78*, 79
Rosthwaite Fell, 75, **78–9**
Rough Crag, 132, 136
Roughten Gill, 12
Ruthwaite Cove, 110, 120
Ruthwaite Lodge, 120
Rydal, 68, 73
Rydal Head, 66, 72
Rydal Water, 73
Rydale, 66, 72

Saddle, The (Blencathra), 11, 12, **14**
Sail Beck, 59

Sail Pass, 62, 63
St John's in the Vale, 109, 203
St Sunday Crag, 66, *66*, *109*
Sallows, 139
Sand Hill, 143, 144, 145
Scafell, 28, *29*, 46, *46*, 55, 75, 77, 96, 128, 138, 170, *172*, **175–85**, *175–85*, 187, 188, 192–4; ascents, 179–83; summit, 184
Scafell Crag, 36, 175–6, 179, 181–3, 184, 187, 189, 192, 194
Scafell Pike, 75, 120, 176, 179, 180, 184, **187–201**, *187–201*; ascents, 190–5; Broad Crag, 198; Great End, 200; Ill Crag, 199; Lingmell, 201; summit, 196–8
Scafell Pinnacle, 181, 183, 184
Scale Force, 123, 125, 128, *129*, 129
Scales Beck, 16
Scales Fell, 4, 10, **11**, *11*, 12
Scales Tarn, 11, 12, **16**, *16*
Scaley Beck, 4, 10, 11
Scar Crags, 59, 62
Scarth Gap, 103, **104**, *104*, 105, 106, 126, 127
Scoat Fell, 170, *171–2*, **171**, 172, 173
Scope End, 55, 57
Scot Rake, 133, 135
Scott, Sir Walter, 16, 118, 120
Seathwaite, 92, 191, 192
Seathwaite Tarn, 37
Seatoller, 52, 76
Shamrock, 168–9
Sharp Edge, 11, 12, **14**, 16
Sheepbone Buttress, 126, *126*
Sheepbone Rake, 126, 127, 128
Shelter Crags, 23, 42, *44*, 45
Side Pike, *149*
Simon's Nick, 33
Sinen Gill, 12, *13*
Skiddaw, 19, *19*, 55, 76, 77, *85*, 106, 128, 138, 200, **203–10**, *203–11*; ascents, 205–8; summit, 209–10
Skiddaw Little Man, 205, **210**, *211*
Slight Side, 179, 188
Solway Firth, 69, 146, 203, 210

Sour Howes, 139
Sourmilk Gill, **93**, 123
Souther Fell, **17**, *19*
Southerndale, 207, 208
Sprinkling Tarn, 96, *190*, 191
Stanger Gill, 78, *78*, 79
Steeple, 163, 170, **172**, *172*
Step, The, 72, *72*
Stickle Breast, 151
Stickle Tarn, 157, *157*, 159, *159*, 161
Sticks Pass, 109, 120, 121
Stockley Bridge, 92, 191, 192
Stone Arthur, 73
Stone Cover, 92, 101
Stonesty Pike, 43, *43*
Stonethwaite, 78
Stoneycroft, 62, 63
Stonythwaite Bridge, 54
Stool End, 22, 23
Straits of Riggindale, 134, *134*, 137, 139
Striding Edge, 14, 109, 110, *111*, 112, **116–17**, *116*, 118, *119*, 120
Sty Head, 77, **92**, 164, 175, 191, **192**, 193, *197*, 200
Sty Head Pass, 90, 92, *92*, 95, 98
Styhead Tarn, 90, 92, 101
Surprise View, *203*
Swinsty Gill, 41, 43
Swirl Hawse, 39
Swirl How, 37–9, *37*, *38*
Swirral Edge, 110, 116, **117**, 120

Tarn at Leaves, *78*, 79
Tarn Crag, *156*, 157
Taylorgill Force, 92
Thirdgillhead Man, 61, 63
Thirlmere, 109, 110, *110*, 111, 112, 113
Thirlspot, 111, 114, 118, 120
Thorn Crag, 150, **154**, 156, 158
Thornthwaite Crag, 133, *134*, 135, 139, *139*
Thornythwaite Fell, 76
Three Shire Stone, 42
Three Tarns, 22, 23, 29, 42, 43, 45
Threlkeld, 7, 8, 9, 12, 17
Threlkeld Common, *1*, 4, 109

Threlkeld Valley, *8*
Tilberthwaite Gill, **39**, *39*
Tongue, The, 120
Tophet Bastion, *98*, 99
Troutbeck, 133, 134, 135, 139

Ullock Pike, 207, 208
Ullswater, 66, *66*, 69, 109, 110, 111, *114*, 118, 121, *121*, 140, 141

Walna Scar Road, 32, **34**, 36
Wandope, 59, 61
Warnscale Beck, 105
Warnscale Bottom, *103*, **105**
Wasdale, 26, 76, *89*, 90, 95, 96, *99*, 158, 175, *176*, 184, 188, 190, 191, 193, 194, 201
Wasdale Head, 89, *90*, 92, 94, 96, 97, 163, 164, 166, 171, 173, *173*, 175, 181, 189, 190, 194
Wastwater, 96, 164, 184, 190, *194*, *201*
West Wall Traverse, 182–3, 192
Westmorland Cairn, 96, *96*
Westmorland Crags, 94
Wether Hill, 140
Wetherlam, *38*, 39
White Napes, 94, 101
White Side, 111, 120, **121**
White Stones (Helvellyn), 113, **114**
White Stones (Skiddaw), 206, *206*
Whiteless Pike, 59, 60, 61, 63
Whiteside, 60, 143, 144, *144*, **145**, **146**, *146*
Whitewater Dash, 208
Whorneyside Force, 23
Wind Gap, 164, 171
Windermere, 28, 46, 69, 138, 139, 149, 158, 159, 163
Windgap Cove, 164, *165*, 170, 171, 172
Windy Gap, 92, *92*, 101
Wordsworth, William, 117, 118
Wrynose Breast, 48
Wrynose Pass, 42, 49
Wythburn, 113, 118

Yew Crag, 52
Yewthwaite Mine, 54
Yoke, 139